ONE BOWL

KELLY McCUNE

ONE BOWL

ONE-DISH MEALS from AROUND the WORLD

Photography by Joyce Oudkerk Pool

CHRONICLE BOOKS
SAN FRANCISCO

Library of Congress Cataloging-in-Publication Data:
McCune, Kelly.
One bowl: one-pot meals from around the world/
Kelly McCune; photographs by Joyce Oudkerk Pool.
          p. cm.
     Includes index.
     ISBN 0-8118-1111-5 (pb)
     1. Entrées (Cookery) 2. Cookery, International. I. Title.
     TX740.M143 1996
     641.8'2—dc20

          96-3395
          CIP

Printed in Hong Kong by Penn & Ink

Distributed in Canada by Raincoast Books
8680 Cambie Street
Vancouver, B.C. V6P 6M9

10 9 8 7 6 5 4 3 2 1

Chronicle Books
275 Fifth Street
San Francisco, CA 94103

Produced by David Barich & Associates
870 Market Street, Suite 690
San Francisco, CA 94102

Design and Production by Barich & Associates
Photography by Joyce Ouderk Pool
Food Styling by Pouké

Special thanks to The Gardener, Acci Gallery and the artists
Bob Pool, Yuri Minarik and Thomas Homann

Acknowledgements

My deepest thanks to Tracy Wynne, for her great ideas, her kitchen savvy, and her enthusiasm for testing, tasting, and perfecting.

Thanks to Mike Fitzgerald for sharing his extensive paella know-how, and to Jerome Vered for his knowledge of all things Chinese: the language, the culture, the food. Lourdes Garcia tasted nearly every dish in this book, and her comments were helpful and always encouraging. Rob Miller of the excellent-palate club was as always a succinct reviewer and most wonderful husband.

CONTENTS

Introduction

The word *casserole* has come to signify both the dish and the cooking pot in which it is prepared. It has meant many things to Americans over the years: In the 1940s and 1950s a casserole was usually a composition of rice or noodles, vegetables, and meat or fish, which was then sprinkled with bread crumbs (or later, crumbled potato chips) and baked to a bubbly doneness. In the 1960s and well into the 1970s a mention of one-pot dishes conjured up images of electric crockpots simmering away on countertops while their owners toiled in downtown skyscrapers. In the 1980s there was a tendency to snub the lowly casserole, as culinary interest turned to quick sautés and grilling. But these one-pot dishes were firmly grounded in a long, trend-resistant tradition that originated from the impulse to combine and consolidate the elements of the meal, to make some of the cooking easier, or to simplify cooking for a crowd. Home cooks have always needed to walk away from the kitchen, leaving the meal to its own devices. In addition, cooking combined ingredients over moderate heat for long periods of time breaks down tough, fibrous vegetables and tenderizes meat, which is good for the budget and the palate.

Nearly every cuisine in the world can claim a one-pot dish that identifies its history, tells some story, or represents an industry important to the country or region. Often a stew or casserole has the humblest origins in a provincial tradition of preparation and ingredients that are fiercely defended and rarely varied. Some of these dishes, such as bouillabaisse or paella, represent the historical backbone of a country—its farming, fishing, or ranching—and were created to feed hungry workers with ingredients at hand. Other dishes, such as *laksa* and sukiyaki, demonstrate the converging influence of different cultures. Many dishes have such a tradition that they are associated with special cooking pots, such as the *couscoussier,* the *paellera,* and the *cassole.*

This book explores classic one-pot dishes, but it also offers many new dishes that are based on flavors and ingredients found around the world. Creating delicious one-pot meals has a certain intrinsic complexity: Every ingredient must be cooked just right, and yet all ingredients must come together in a well-defined harmony. The elements of the dish must be distinct, retaining their own personalities and bright colors.

I have tried to be true to the traditional preparation of and ingredients in most of the classic one-pot dishes, but I have reduced the oil wherever possible and, in recognition of our busy lives, have streamlined preparation to save time. Because ingredients must often be cooked separately before they come together in the final dish, you may end up with more than one dirty pot in your sink. "One-pot" doesn't always denote simplicity or speed, but these dishes are fulfilling to make and delicious to eat. One-pot meals are comforting and wholesome; they are meant to be shared with others. They celebrate abundance, but they also show that from a few humble ingredients, a dish can be created that emerges as something gloriously unexpected.

The Pots

Throughout the world of food and cooking there are pots, pans, pottery, casseroles, and dishes that are inextricably linked to the meal that is cooked in them. Every cuisine has at least one favorite one-pot dish, a recipe that has been shared and protected through generations, with techniques and ingredients that have been refined and cemented in time, and cookware deemed essential to its preparation. In current English usage *casserole* means both the pot and the meal, food cooked in one pot or dish and served from it. The *couscoussier* combines the cooking pot for the stew with the steamer for the couscous grains. It is hard to imagine paella cooked in anything other than the lightweight, large, double-handled *paellera* that gives the dish its name. Earthenware and metal pots have been used as cooking tools for thousands of years. Clay was the first material molded into cookware—it was immediate, could be made to suit the needs of the cook, and could be replaced with ease. Throughout culinary history, pottery has been ideal for cooking because it warms up slowly and maintains an even temperature. However, it is not well suited to high-heat cooking. Metal, particularly iron, has been favored for its ability to withstand high, direct heat and for its even cooking. Metal cookware is now so ubiquitous that we think of it first when outfitting a kitchen.

Bean Pot

A lidded casserole with a fat bottom and narrow top, usually made of earthenware or stoneware, has been called a *bean pot* in the United States since Puritan times. The tapered top reduces evaporation, and the pottery bakes the beans slowly and evenly, perfect for keeping them moist and tender.

Brazier

A *brazier* is a low casserole, double-handled, with a heavy bottom. The thick bottom promotes an initial even browning of meats and vegetables before liquid is added for braising on the stovetop. Braziers are designed for maximum evaporation and reduction, but they come with a lid for retaining moisture. These pots look like sauté pans without the long handle, and they may simply be labeled as such or as casseroles.

Casserole

In French a *casserole* is simply a saucepan, but in English it describes both the dish and the pot in which it is cooked. It has also become a term that encompasses a large family of cooking vessels of many different shapes and functions. Many of the recipes that are habitually called casseroles are actually cooked in shallow glass or pottery baking dishes. A true casserole is generally a heavy pot with a tight-fitting lid, suitable for the oven or the stovetop. It typically has two handles on either side rather than one long handle like its cousin, the saucepan. This handle design makes it easy to fit a casserole in the oven. Because casseroles tend to be more squat than they are tall, they can accommodate larger cuts of meats and vegetables. The tight lid keeps moisture in, a desirable feature for long, slow cooking. Most casseroles have at least a 3- to 5-quart capacity, but they are available in larger sizes. Casseroles are made from cast iron, stainless steel, aluminum, enameled cast iron, lined copper, earthenware, porcelain, and stoneware.

Cassole

A *cassole* was the earthenware pot in which *cassoulet*, a French combination of beans and meats, was originally prepared; the pot lent the dish its name. Now the *marmite*, a very similar pot, is more commonly used for cassoulet.

Cast Iron Pot

The process of separating iron from its ore was developed only about 4,000 years ago, and its immediate use was not for cooking. Eventually, however, industrious ironworkers found it to be a good material to cast into cookware (pots were made of earthenware up to that point), and the creation of iron pots of all sizes and shapes abounded. Iron pots are excellent cooking vessels because they heat up quickly, retain the heat evenly, and can be used over very high heat for searing and browning. Their drawbacks are that they rust easily and pit over time, and they can absorb odors and flavors, leaving behind the vaguest reference to the food most recently cooked in them. Cast iron pots are heavy and can withstand even the worst treatment. They are well suited to long-cooking stews, both on the stovetop and in the oven. Enameled cast iron makes a wonderful cooking pot; it has the benefits of iron without the problems of rust and pitting. Enamel is sprayed onto the iron and baked on, producing a tough, extremely well-bonded finish on the pot that can be chipped, but not easily. The enamel surface is so hard that it absorbs no food odors or flavors, and any stains can be scoured out with a gentle grainy cleanser.

Chinese Firepot

Also called a Mongolian hot pot, the *Chinese firepot* is much like a fondue pot, but the traditional firepot has a more elaborate charcoal-burning structure. The firepot must be ventilated properly because charcoal produces carbon monoxide fumes, which can build up indoors. The basis of the dish is the broth, kept bubbling over the heat, into which each diner dips thin slices of meat, vegetables, and ultimately noodles to cook them. A variety of dipping sauces and condiments are served with the meal, and by the end the broth, now deliciously flavored, is served with the noodles as a soup. Chinese markets are the best place to find firepots.

Clay Pot

Clay is the material that was used for the first cooking vessels. It was readily available and low tech, and could be easily replaced when broken. Earthen pots can be fired at various temperatures; the higher the heat, the harder the piece. Clay or earthenware pots are fired at a relatively low heat and thus are fragile and porous. Glazed earthenware is harder and not porous on the glazed surface. Stoneware is quite hard and not at all porous. Porcelain is the hardest pottery, with a glass-like surface. Unglazed clay pots can be soaked in water before use, so that they retain moisture and minimize the amount of fat needed for cooking. They can also be rubbed on the inside with garlic to create a "seal." Glazed clay pots do not need to be soaked.

Clay pots heat up slowly but retain their heat evenly and for a long time, making them well suited to long, slow, moist cooking. Some cheaply made clay pots may contain lead-based glazes, so buy them from a reputable seller. The clay pots described in this chapter are the bean pot, cassole, daubière, marmite, olla, sandpot, stewpot, terrine, and tajine.

Cocotte

A French term for casserole, *cocotte* describes any number of straight-sided, round or oval lidded pots that are used for making stews and for long-cooked meals.

Couscoussier

The two-level *couscoussier* is perfectly designed for cooking a flavorful, aromatic *tajine,* or stew, in the bottom section and for steaming the grains of semolina in the top section. This design imitates the early use of a woven basket for holding the couscous over the steaming stew in the pot beneath. Like the basket, the top of the couscoussier is perforated to allow steam to pass through the couscous and escape, a technique that keeps the delicate grains from getting mushy. A couscoussier should be lightweight and is usually made of aluminum. Many cookware stores carry couscoussiers, but they are rather expensive. Look for less expensive pots in markets specializing in Middle Eastern foods, where you may be able to obtain one by special order. Because the couscous available in our markets is precooked, long steaming is no longer needed. Thus a couscoussier has become a more decorative than strictly functional implement.

Daubière

The *daubière* gets its name from the French dish *daube*, a somewhat generic term for stew. This stew-pot is traditionally made of earthenware or stoneware and has a bulbous bottom and narrower top. This design allows the stew to cook slowly and gently with little loss of moisture; the effect is to tenderize and enhance the flavor of the ingredients. The classic daubière has a single short handle for stovetop use, as well as two side handles for lifting the pot in and out of the oven. The lip of the lid and the rim of the pot are left unglazed to create as tight a seal as possible. The daubière is similar in design and intention to the bean pot and to what the English call a stew jar.

Doufeu

The French pot *doufeu,* so named for gentle (*doux*) and fire (*feu*), is a metal casserole that historically was intended for the gentlest cooking over a wood fire. Its flat, depressed lid was designed to hold hot coals, so that the food would cook gently and evenly from above and below. The design is now used as a way to control moisture loss from the pot. The pan-shaped lid is filled with ice or cold water, which encourages liquid to condense on the inside of the lid and drip back into the pot instead of evaporating. The doufeu can also be used as a straightforward casserole.

Dutch Oven

Also called a kettle, the *Dutch oven* is an old-fashioned, heavy iron pot. Old ones can sometimes be found with three stout little legs that supported the pot over its bed of coals. The metal handle was originally used to hang the pot from a swing-out hook over the fire. Nowadays, Dutch oven is another term for certain heavy, round or oval cast iron casseroles.

Marmite

The beautiful *marmite* is the cousin of the daubière and the bean pot. Its sides are straight, or only slightly tapered or rounded, and it has two handles and a well-fitted lid. Marmites are made of earthenware or sometimes stoneware; they are unglazed or partly glazed. Traditionally, the inside of an unglazed marmite is rubbed liberally with garlic, the oil of which acts to "seal" the pottery. Marmites are used less on the stove-top (where very low heat or a flame tamer is required) and more for composed dishes, such as cassoulet, that bake slowly in the oven.

Olla

The Mexican *olla* is a large, rounded pot of glazed or partly glazed earthenware, used for the slow cooking of beans, in particular, and for other dishes such as *birria,* the spicy Mexican soup made with shredded goat or mutton stewed with vegetables and lots of chilies.

Paellera

Also called a paella or paella pan, a *paellera* is the large, double-handled skillet from which the Spanish dish *paella* got its name. Its two handles make it easy to carry a full pan of paella. With its saffron-laced rice, chicken, and seafood, paella is the perfect dish for a group. A 15-inch pan (measured at the top rim) will serve eight to ten people. A paellera need not be made of any material fancier than lightweight untreated steel, which can be seasoned in the oven with a light coating of vegetable oil. The pan will continue to season as you use it. Because paella is always cooked uncovered, a paellera never has a lid. Good sources for an inexpensive paellera are restaurant supply or discount import stores.

Pot

Pot is the most generic term for metal or earthenware cooking vessels that are used on the stovetop or in the oven. For most people, however, a pot has one long handle, while a casserole or stewpot is larger and has two short handles.

Sandpot

Also called a Chinese clay pot, sandy pot, or earthen pot, the *sandpot* is an earthenware cooking pot named for the sandy, grainy texture of the unfinished clay on the outside. The inside of the pot is glazed. Sandpots come in various sizes, all with lids. Many sandpots have a wire frame to help prevent chipping and cracking. Sandpots are for low-heat, slow, stovetop cooking, and a flame tamer or diffuser is needed for electric burners. Avoid putting a hot pot on a cold surface or an empty pot on the heat, and do not use a sandpot in a microwave. The attractive earthiness of this pot makes it a nice dish to serve from as well. Sandpots should not be expensive; they can be found in Asian markets and some cookware stores.

Stewpot

Stewpot is another name for casserole, a covered pot for stewing, but it may also refer to a daubiére.

Stockpot

The *stockpot* is a tall pot with a lid. It differs from a casserole or stewpot in being taller than it is wide, a shape that minimizes evaporation when making stock from bones. Stockpots are also often made to be lighter in weight than casseroles or stewpots. The bottom of a stockpot, however, should be thick, heavy, and highly conductive, to evenly simmer the stock from the bottom up through the contents of the pot.

Sukiyaki Pot

Also called *sukiyaki nabe*, the *sukiyaki pot* is a shallow pot or pan that is always made of some kind of metal for quickly searing beef and vegetables before the broth is added. Cast iron is an excellent choice because it heats evenly and holds its heat well. Sukiyaki is cooked at the table, so these pots are often very attractively cast, forming part of the overall aesthetic of this wonderful meal.

Tajine

Also spelled tajin or tagine, a *tajine* is an attractive North African pot with a conical lid. It is used for preparing stews, which cook slowly on the stovetop or in the oven. The word *tajine* doubles for both stew and stewpot. Tajines are made of glazed or unglazed earthenware, usually fairly thick, to accommodate the long cooking required to thicken dried beans, peas, and lentils and to tenderize meat. Use a flame tamer for stovetop cooking. Tajines are difficult to find but may be available (by special order) through markets specializing in North African or Middle Eastern foods.

Terrine

A *terrine*, with its roots in the French word *terre*, or earth, is traditionally an earthenware casserole, either oval or rectangular in shape. A terrine is also the dish cooked in this pot: a firm, composed dish that is served directly from the pot, such as some pâtés, items cooked in aspic or in a crust, or minced and baked meats or fish. The vent hole in the top allows the steam to escape so that the terrine bakes rather than stews. Terrines also can be used as oven casseroles.

The Pantry

Cooking authentic dishes from other countries often requires a search for some rather uncommon ingredients. Sometimes nothing but the called-for ingredient will do. Many cities, both large and small, have ethnic markets, and gourmet markets are opening every day. Mail order is another good source for unusual ingredients, but it requires planning ahead. If all else fails in your search for a particular ingredient, call a local restaurant that serves the type of food you are preparing and ask for suggestions!

Arborio Rice

Arborio, a short-grain Italian white rice, is the classic ingredient for risotto. Short-grain rice has fat, oval grains with a high starch content, which makes them cling together when cooked. Paella is also made with short-grain rice, and although Spanish paella rice is sold in the United States, Arborio is more common and makes an excellent substitute. Other names for short-grain rice are pearl and *mochi* (Japanese).

Banh Pho

Banh generally describes most of the Vietnamese rice pastas. There are all sorts: rice papers, short thick noodles, noodle sheets, and spaghetti-sized rice noodles, to name a few. *Banh pho* more specifically refers to the noodle used in *pho,* the delicious Vietnamese soup of incredibly fresh and flavorful ingredients. Although fresh rice noodles are available in Asian markets, dried rice noodles (or sticks, as they are most often labeled) are more widely available and can be used in place of fresh.

Basmati Rice

Basmati is one of several varieties of aromatic long-grain rice used throughout the world. It is becoming more available in supermarkets in the United States, and is an essential ingredient for any Indian rice-based dish. Its sweet perfume and nutty flavor are unmistakable, and its long, thin grain has the most delicate texture. It is imported from India, where it is grown at the foot of the Himalayas and then aged to reduce moisture content and intensify flavor. Serve basmati rice with Indian and Middle Eastern dishes.

Blacan

Also called *belacan* or *blachan,* or *kapi* in Thai cuisine, *blacan* is dried shrimp paste, which in one form or another is a common ingredient in Southeast Asian cooking. Its extremely pungent odor and intense saltiness add a complex flavor to Asian dishes that is unlike any other, and nothing can be used as a substitute. Blacan is the Malaysian version of this staple, and it comes in small cakes or blocks. Although shrimp paste should be cooked before it is used, dishes often consist of a *rempah* (spice blend) of ingredients that are bubbled in a skillet for several minutes before being added to the sauce or soup, a process that cooks the paste at the same time.

Bouquet Garni

The classic *bouquet garni* consists of parsley, thyme, and bay leaf tied together at the stems or bound into a cheesecloth bag. Bouquets garnis are used to flavor broth, soups, and stews. Herbs bundled in this way infuse a dish with flavor and can be easily removed at the end of cooking.

Cardamom

Cardamom is an aromatic spice used in many parts of the world. Some cuisines employ it in baked goods; in many countries it is used in savory dishes. Indian food is almost incomplete without cardamom, and its whitish, green, or black pods are often used whole in Indian dishes. The seeds contain the flavor and can be used whole. If ground cardamom is called for, the best bet is to grind the seeds using a mortar and pestle. The flavor of packaged ground cardamom lacks the intensity and sweetness of freshly ground.

Chili Powder

Chili powder is the term used for the seasoning mix—usually ground red chilies, cumin, oregano, garlic, and coriander—most often used in chili. There are many purveyors of chili powder, each with a claim to excellence, each with a different flavor. Ground red chilies, made from nothing but ground dried chili peppers, are often confused with chili powder. Cayenne pepper is made from very hot ground red chilies. Ground *ancho* chilies and ground red chilies from New Mexico are milder varieties.

Chilies

This selection represents only some of the many varieties of fresh and dried *chilies* available in the market. When you are buying fresh chilies, look for shiny skins with unclouded color and no blemishes. Dried chilies should have a bright color, not a gray, dried-out cast. Removing the seeds and whitish ribs inside the chili will diminish its heat by almost 80 percent, but take care not to touch your eyes when handling chilies. If you are in doubt about the heat of a particular variety, ask the greengrocer for advice.

Anaheim: Also called California or long green. A fleshy green, smooth 6-inch chili with a mild flavor.
Ancho: A sweet dried *poblano* chili.
Chilaca: A long, twisted, dark brown chili, most commonly used in its dry form, the *pasilla*.
Chipotle: The dried, smoked form of a large *jalapeño*. Available in cans packed in *adobo* sauce.
Fresno: A small red chili, often called a red jalapeño. Sweet, with a medium-hot flavor.
Guajillo: A dried red chili with a sweet, not-too-hot flavor.

Habanero: A small, fat crinkled ball of a chili, and one of the hottest chilies around. Can be found in colors ranging from yellow to dark purple and is also available dried.
Jalapeño: Small 2- to 3-inch chilies, hot but not excessively so. They can be green or red (sweeter), and are fairly easy to find fresh.
New Mexico, green: Also called long green. A 6-inch green chili with a few more bends and folds than the smoother Anaheim. It has a clear, hot-but-not-too-hot flavor and is excellent fresh or roasted.
New Mexico, red: Also called *Colorado*. A flavorful chili like its green cousin, it is also available dried and in varying degrees of hotness.
Pasilla: A dried chilaca, and one of the primary ingredients in the rich Mexican sauce, *mole*.
Poblano: A purplish-green 4- to 5-inch chili. It is best roasted and has a clean hot flavor with a hint of sweetness.
Serrano: A little red or green chili, the most widely available hot fresh chili in American markets. It can be used as a substitute for the Thai chili, but the amount needs to be doubled.
Thai: A tiny, thin red or green chili, the most commonly used in Southeast Asian cooking. It can be found in Asian markets.

Chinese Black Beans

Chinese black beans, a salty seasoning as old as Chinese cooking, is made of fermented soybeans preserved in salt. Also called salty black beans or fermented black beans, they can be found packed in plastic or jars in Chinese markets. Keep them tightly wrapped and store them in the refrigerator for up to a year. Black bean paste or sauce is made from ground fermented black beans mixed with a little sugar and oil, and can be used as a substitute.

Chinese Black Mushrooms

Woodsy and rich, *Chinese black mushrooms* add a unique flavor to dishes. These mushrooms are called *shiitakes* in Japan and can be found dried, in packages, and sometimes fresh. The dried mushrooms have a more intense flavor, perfect in some stews and soups. Soak dried mushrooms in warm water for 30 minutes before using them.

Chinese Broccoli

Chinese broccoli is the green stalk vegetable that is often served at dim sum restaurants, braised and doused with soy sauce. It has a delicious, full flavor and crunchy texture that are far from the usual qualities of the broccoli found in most supermarkets. Fresh Chinese broccoli has perky leaves and possibly little flowers, a firm stem, and no dry cracks or bruises. It is available in any Asian market.

Chinese Rice Wine

Sherrylike in color and flavor, *Chinese rice wine* is fermented from rice. It should have a good flavor and aroma—the best ones come from the city of Shaoxing. Dry sherry can be used as a substitute.

Chorizo

In the sausage world, *chorizo* has a flavor all its own. It is made from either freshly ground pork (Mexican) or smoked pork (Spanish) mixed with myriad seasonings, such as garlic, dried chilies, cumin, oregano, and coriander. Remove the casing and crumble the coarsely ground meat into a pan for browning, or cook the sausage in the casing if it is firm and you want pieces.

Cilantro

Also called Chinese parsley or coriander, *cilantro* has lacy leaves that look a little like parsley, but its flavor is pungent and citrusy, and very distinct. Cilantro is sold in bunches, which should be fresh and bright green. The entire plant can be used, including the tender stems. Cilantro is used in many cuisines throughout the world, and its popularity is on the rise in this country because of our love for Mexican cooking. Cilantro is available in many supermarkets and gourmet grocery stores.

Cipollini

Meaning "little onions," *cipollini* from Italy are deliciously sweet, particularly when glazed and then stewed. They are about 1 inch in diameter and are somewhat flat, with yellow skin. To make them easier to peel, drop them in boiling water for 3 minutes, drain them, and when they are cool enough to handle, trim off just the root end and peel off the papery skins.

Coconut Milk

Coconut milk can be found in some supermarkets and in any Asian grocery store. It is most commonly sold in cans, although it is sometimes available frozen. Coconut milk is made by simmering shredded coconut with water, straining it, and then squeezing as much milk from the meat as possible. *Thick coconut milk* is the term for the milk straight from the can, after the cream on the top is mixed into the rest (done by shaking the can vigorously before opening it). *Thin coconut milk* is the milk from the can diluted 1 to 1 with water.

Couscous

The "pasta" of North Africa, *couscous* is a tiny grain made from ground durum wheat (semolina) that has been lightly moistened and then rolled until dry and granular. Almost all the couscous available in the United States has been precooked and needs only to be moistened with liquid and steeped, covered, for 5 to 7 minutes to plump it.

Crème Fraîche

Ripened cream is a staple ingredient in French cooking. Cream is able to ripen naturally in France, since it is unpasteurized; when kept at room temperature, the cream is thickened by the bacteria it contains. *Crème fraîche* has a slight tanginess, less pronounced than that of sour cream. It is wonderful stirred into soups and sauces because of its creaminess, and because it does not curdle. *Crème fraîche* can be made at home by adding 2 tablespoons of buttermilk to 1 cup of whipping cream and allowing this to stand at room temperature, covered, overnight. Stir and refrigerate.

Fava Beans

Fava beans are a North African bean, popular in Middle Eastern and Mediterranean cuisines. They are sometimes available fresh, in pods, but the skins of the beans themselves need to be removed by blanching prior to cooking. Dried favas have a firm texture and nutty flavor; they are delicious in stews and tajines. They should be soaked overnight before they are cooked.

Galangal

Also called *galanga, kha,* Thai or Siamese ginger, *galangal* is a rhizome that looks very much like ginger but has a smoother, thinner skin. It is used like ginger as a seasoning in Southeast Asian cooking. It has less tang but a more peppery flavor than ginger. It can be found fresh in Asian markets. Dried galangal is an acceptable substitute; it should be soaked in warm water before it is used.

Ghee

Also called *usli ghee, ghee* is a type of clarified butter used in Indian cooking. All the milk solids have been removed from regular butter, so that it becomes a kind of "butter oil" that can be used at high temperatures without burning. To make your own ghee, melt a stick of butter over low heat. Spoon off the foam on the top. Pour the melted butter into a glass bowl and allow it to cool completely. Spoon the oil off the top of the hardened solids—this oil is the ghee. It can be stored refrigerated up to 3 months.

Harissa

Harissa, a spicy hot chili sauce from North Africa, is made from red chilies, garlic, olive oil, and assorted spices. It is served alongside couscous and can be used in other North African dishes as well. Harissa is available in jars or cans in Middle Eastern markets.

Hominy

Hominy is one of the many foods indigenous to America, and the name probably comes from the Algonquin word *rockahominy,* for dried cornmeal. Corn kernels are first dried, then soaked in a lime solution to remove the hull and germ, and cooked. The result is a plump, tender corn kernel with a cooked corn flavor. Hominy is available canned, frozen, and dried. Easiest to use is the canned hominy, which needs only to be drained and heated.

Kaffir Lime

The *kaffir lime* is a bumpy, thick-skinned lime used extensively in Thai cooking. The leaves and rind, rather than the juice or flesh, are used. When grating a kaffir lime, use a fine grater and remove only the green skin, not the white pith underneath. The leaves have two parts, like an 8, though they snap in two easily and may be separated when you buy them. One leaf is really the two parts together, with the tough spine trimmed out. Kaffir limes are available in markets specializing in Thai food. They are best fresh, but both the lime and the leaves can be found frozen. Dried kaffir lime rind is bitter and therefore not a good substitute.

Kalamata Olives

Greek *kalamata olives* are oval and dark purple, almost black. They have a rich flavor with no bitterness. Buy them in bulk, if possible, from a Greek, Middle Eastern, or gourmet market.

Kapi

Similar to Malaysian blacan, *kapi* is the Thai version of shrimp paste. Small shrimp are salted, dried, and ground. Kapi varies in color, from gray to brownish, and in texture, from soft to firm and dry. Even though kapi is used in small amounts, its unique flavor is characteristic of Thai cooking.

Laksa Noodles

Laksa noodles are a kind of rice vermicelli. These very thin noodles are used in the Malaysian curry noodle soup *laksa*.

Lemongrass

Lemongrass is the single flavoring that may define Thai cooking. Thai food cannot be prepared at home without it, so resort to dried lemongrass only if absolutely necessary. Lemongrass is an herb that looks very much like a green onion with drier, tougher leaves. It has a lemony flavor and aroma and a fibrous texture. It is usually finely minced and added to dishes, or used in pastes. Remove the toughest outer layer, and use only the whitish part above the root (2 to 3 inches). The leaves are not used.

Malaysian Curry Powder

Although *Malaysian curry powder* is made up of many of the same ingredients as are found in Indian curry powder, the result is slightly different. Malaysian curry powder is sweet and hot, with a more pronounced anise flavor. It can be found in Asian markets; if unavailable, use Indian curry powder as a substitute.

Metaxa

Metaxa is a smooth, dark Greek brandy with a unique sweet, almost piney flavor. Metaxa is the name for both the brandy and the maker. Serve it like a brandy or use it as a flavoring in Greek dishes.

Mirin

Japanese *mirin* is a smooth, ever-so-slightly thickened wine (though it contains almost no alcohol), fermented from glutinous rice. It is used only in cooking. Mirin can be found in many supermarkets in the Asian foods section.

Nam Pla

Nam pla, a Thai specialty, is related to *kapi*. Nam pla is the liquid produced when salted fish or shrimp are sun-dried and drained. It has an intensely salty, fishy flavor and is used to season sauces and pastes. Look for nam pla in markets specializing in Thai foods. *Nuoc mam*, the Vietnamese version, can be used as a substitute.

Nuoc Mam

Nuoc mam is the Vietnamese version of nam pla.

Pecorino Cheese

A hard grating cheese from Italy, *pecorino* is much like Parmesan but is made from sheep's milk rather than cow's milk. Pecorino has a sharper flavor and tastes a bit saltier.

Porcini Mushrooms

Also called *cèpes*, *porcinis* are related to wild mushrooms and have an earthy, almost smoky flavor. They are sometimes, though rarely, available fresh; more often they are available dried. Look for dried mushrooms that are mostly intact, not broken up. They should be pale brown. Although dried porcinis are quite expensive by the pound, a few ounces goes a long way. Soak the dried mushrooms in warm water for half an hour or so before using them, and add the soaking liquid to the dish if possible.

Rice Noodles, Rice Sticks, Rice Vermicelli

Rice noodles are made from rice flour rather than wheat flour. In Asian markets rice noodles are available fresh or dried. The fresh noodles are stiff, but they do not need to be soaked before cooking. Dried rice noodles are whitish, becoming nearly translucent when cooked. *Rice sticks* are dried noodles that range in size from about spaghetti width to 1/4 inch across. *Rice vermicelli* are very thin and fragile dried noodles, and they cook in no time. Rice noodles are used in noodle dishes and soups throughout China, Japan, and Southeast Asia. For instance, *bahn pho* noodles are used in the Vietnamese soup *pho,* and *laksa* noodles are used in the Malaysian soup laksa.

Saffron

An extremely expensive spice, *saffron* is actually the stigma of the *Crocus sativus,* culled from hundreds of thousands of flowers. The best saffron comes from crocus flowers grown in Tunisia, Spain, and India; Mexican saffron is not as intense. Avoid powdered saffron, which may have been mixed with dried marigold petals. Saffron adds color—a very distinctive orange yellow—to dishes, as well as a unique earthy, rich flavor. Buy it in strands, and crush it with a mortar and pestle or with the back of a wooden spoon, as needed.

Sake

Japanese rice wine, *sake,* is the favored alcoholic drink in Japan. It is a slightly sweet wine made from fermented rice and has a low alcohol content. It is also used in Japanese cooking. Many liquor stores carry different brands of sake, and markets specializing in Japanese food carry it as well.

Sambal

A *sambal* is a Southeast Asian salsa, or sauce. The simplest sambal is a mixture of chilies and salt, but numerous varieties also include different spices, sugar, and such seasonings as shrimp paste. Sambals are used as spicy condiments to accompany Indonesian, Malaysian, and Indian dishes.

Shiitake Mushrooms

Also called Chinese black mushroom, *shiitakes* have a delicious, woodsy taste. Originally from China and Japan, they are now cultivated in the United States and so are much easier to find fresh. Dried shiitakes are also widely available. Soak them in warm water for 20 minutes before cooking them.

Shirataki Noodles

Made from the starch of a tuber called Devil's Tongue, *shirataki noodles* are often labeled yam noodles. They are translucent and somewhat rubbery and absorb any flavors with which they come in contact. Shirataki noodles are available packed in water in 1-pound tubs, refrigerated, in markets that specialize in Japanese food.

Sour Cherries, Dried

Dried sour cherries are stocked with the raisins and dried fruit in some supermarkets, or in health food stores or ethnic markets. Both sweet and sour cherries are dried; the sour variety is more suited to savory cooking.

Star Anise

Each of the eight star-shaped points of the beautiful *star anise* pod holds a tiny flavorful seed. This spice is used frequently in Chinese and Southeast Asian cooking and is best purchased whole rather than ground. Star anise has a flavor reminiscent of anise (a licorice taste), but it is more pungent. It should be used sparingly, and when used whole it can be removed at any time during cooking.

Thai Eggplant

Small eggplant varieties such as *Thai eggplant* can range from as small as a bean to egg size. The most common variety is the small, round, egg-sized eggplant that is off-white with green stripes; this eggplant may also be all white or have a deep purple color. Thai eggplant is sweet and tender and does not need to be salted and drained. It cooks quickly and retains its delicate flavor. A long, narrow Japanese or Oriental eggplant can be substituted.

Tofu

Tofu is made from curdled soy milk, which is drained and pressed into cakes, a process very similar to cheese making. But tofu is more like a palette than cheese, because it takes on the flavor of whatever it is cooked with. It comes in soft, silky textures and in firmer, drier textures. Fresh tofu is packaged in water in 1-pound tubs, in the refrigerated section of most supermarkets. To keep tofu fresh, change this water periodically.

Fried tofu is tofu that has been sliced into strips, triangles, or cakes; deep-fried; and packed in flat cellophane-wrapped packages, also refrigerated. It can be freshened by refrying or used directly from the package. Keep fried tofu refrigerated.

One-Pot Dishes

BOUILLABAISSE WITH ROUILLE AND GARLIC CROUTONS

Bouillabaisse is a fish stew with affiliations all along the French coast of the Mediterranean. In the Provence city of Marseilles, which claims the original title of ownership, it is said that the fishermen created this meal-in-a-kettle on the beach after a long day with the nets. Like all great working-class dishes, bouillabaisse began as a way to use the rejects—the unsold or ugliest and least salable fish (such as racasse, or scorpion fish)—and was perfected day after working day. To make bouillabaisse in the true improvisational spirit of the French fishermen, choose the freshest fish and shellfish from what is available at your local fish market, and use this recipe as a template. Try to combine firm fish, such as monkfish or swordfish, with medium-textured fish such as halibut, rockfish, grouper, cod, sea bass, or striped bass, and then with more fragile fish such as red snapper, John Dory, pompano, sole, whiting, flounder, sea trout, or porgy. Mussels, clams, lobster, and shrimp are fine to use also. The more, the merrier in the bouillabaisse pot!

FISH STOCK

The essence of a great fresh fish stew is homemade fish stock.

Rinse the fish bones and shrimp shells and place them in a stockpot.

Add the water, wine, Pernod or Ricard, onion, carrot, parsley, and peppercorns. Bring to a boil, reduce the heat and simmer, uncovered, for 45 minutes. Strain the stock through a colander lined with several layers of cheesecloth. Discard the solids and reserve the stock.

BOUILLABAISSE

Heat the olive oil in a large pot over medium heat. Cook the onion, leek, fennel, and carrot until wilted and browning, about 8 minutes. Add the garlic and sauté another minute. Add the tomatoes, thyme, tarragon, saffron, orange rind, and fish stock and simmer, partly covered, for 30 minutes. Prepare the croutons and rouille.

Purée half of the soup in a food processor or blender with the tomato paste. Pour it back into the pot, and season to taste with salt and pepper. Keep warm.

In a covered saucepan, steam the mussels in a half inch of the reserved fish stock until they open. Discard any that do not open. Keep the steamed mussels warm until needed.

Bring the soup to a simmer. Add the fish, putting the firmest fish in first and after several minutes adding the less firm fish and the shrimp. Altogether the fish should cook in 10 to 12 minutes. Ladle the soup into bowls, and divide the warm mussels among the servings. Put a crouton on the side of each bowl and a dollop of crème fraîche and rouille in the center. Sprinkle a few reserved fennel leaves on top. Pass the extra croutons and rouille.

SERVES 8

FISH STOCK
1 to 2 pounds fish bones
24 shells from medium-sized
   shrimp
10 cups water
1 cup dry white wine
⅓ cup Pernod or Ricard
1 onion, quartered
1 carrot, quartered
4 parsley sprigs
10 peppercorns

BOUILLABAISSE
3 tablespoons olive oil
1 large onion, chopped
1 leek, white part, chopped
1 fennel bulb, cored and green
   tops removed (reserve some of
   the feathery leaves), chopped
1 carrot, peeled and chopped
4 large garlic cloves, peeled and
   minced
3 large tomatoes, peeled, seeded,
   and chopped
1 teaspoon fresh thyme leaves,
   or ½ teaspoon dried thyme
1 teaspoon chopped fresh
   tarragon, or ½ teaspoon dried
   tarragon
⅛ teaspoon crushed saffron
   threads (see Pantry)
½ teaspoon grated orange rind

8 cups fish stock (see recipe)
4 tablespoons tomato paste
Salt and freshly ground black
  pepper, to taste
24 mussels, scrubbed and
  debearded
2 pounds filleted white fish, bones
  removed, in bite-sized pieces
24 medium-sized shrimp, shelled
  and deveined
Garlic croutons (see recipe)
Crème fraîche (see Pantry)
Rouille (see recipe)

GARLIC CROUTONS
1 baguette
Olive oil
2 garlic cloves, peeled and root ends
  trimmed

ROUILLE
1 red bell pepper
3 garlic cloves, peeled and chopped
1 slice of sturdy white bread, crust
  removed
2 tablespoons fish stock (see recipe,
  above)
1 egg yolk
Pinch of crushed saffron threads
½ to ¾ cup fruity olive oil
Salt, to taste
Cayenne pepper, to taste

GARLIC CROUTONS

Slice the bread on the diagonal into 1/2-inch ovals to make about 24 croutons. Toast the slices under a broiler, turning once. Immediately brush one side of each slice lightly with the olive oil. Lightly rub the oiled side of the bread with the raw garlic, just enough to give the bread a hint of garlic flavor.

ROUILLE

This sauce, named for the French word for "rust" because of its reddish color, is a spicy Provençal sauce—like aïoli but with roasted red pepper added.

Roast the red pepper over the burner of a gas range or in a broiler. When the skin is black, place the pepper in a paper bag and allow to steam for 5 minutes. Scrape off the blackened skin, and remove and discard the stem and seeds. Purée the pepper and the garlic in a food processor. Moisten the bread with the fish stock, then add it to the puréed pepper mixture along with the egg yolk and saffron; process until smooth. With the processor running, add the oil in a steady stream until the rouille is smooth and has the texture of thickened cream.

Season to taste with salt and cayenne pepper, and refrigerate until needed.

LAMB TAJINE WITH DATES AND ALMONDS

A tajine is a flavorful North African stew and the name of its cooking pot as well. Tajines can contain lamb, chicken, or other meats, fish, or only vegetables. They can be thick and slightly sweet or thinner and more souplike. The variations are as endless as there are cooks to think them up. The tajine in which these stews are cooked is typically a squat clay pot with a conical lid resembling a hat. Tajines can be served with couscous or rice, or with lots of warmed pita bread and hummus or baba ghanoush.

Preheat the oven to 325°. Heat half the oil in a large, heavy skillet (if you are using a tajine) or in a metal casserole. Sauté the lamb in batches, adding more oil as needed, until it is well browned on all sides. Remove to a plate. When all the lamb is browned, sauté the onion until golden, about 7 minutes. Add the garlic and cook another minute.

Put the browned lamb and onions in the tajine, or back into the casserole, and add the carrots, cumin, cinnamon, coriander, ginger, caraway seeds, cilantro, and water. Stir to combine. Cover and cook for 1 hour in the preheated oven. Add the dates and cook another 20 minutes. Before serving, stir in the lemon juice, season to taste with salt and pepper, and sprinkle with the almonds and cilantro.

SERVES 6

4 tablespoons olive oil

2 pounds lamb stew meat, in ½-inch cubes

3 medium onions, chopped

4 garlic cloves, minced to a paste

2 large carrots, peeled and coarsely grated

2 teaspoons ground cumin

2 teaspoons ground cinnamon

2 teaspoons ground coriander

1 teaspoon ground ginger

½ teaspoon caraway seeds

¼ cup chopped fresh cilantro (see Pantry)

2½ cups water

1 cup pitted and quartered dates, about 16 whole dates

2 tablespoons lemon juice

Salt and freshly ground black pepper, to taste

½ cup slivered almonds, lightly toasted

Chopped fresh cilantro, for garnish

PASTA E FAGIOLI WITH WHITE BEANS, TORTELLINI, AND WILD MUSHROOMS

The pairing of beans and pasta is almost as old as the hills of Rome. Traditionally, pasta e fagioli *combines tagliatelle pasta, or even homemade pasta "remnants," with either cannellini or borlotti white beans, but even these general rules vary by region. This version is a bean soup with tortellini, flavored with sweet fennel and earthy porcini mushrooms.*

Rinse the beans in a colander and pick out any stones. Soak overnight in plenty of cold water. Drain and set aside.

Rinse the fennel bulbs and cut off the green tops. Pull off enough of the feathery leaves to make ⅓ cup, and set aside in the refrigerator. Slice each fennel bulb in half lengthwise, cut out the hard core, and thinly slice the halves. In a large pot, gently cook the bacon until it releases its fat. Add the sliced fennel and onion and sauté over medium heat until both are wilted and beginning to turn a golden color, about 10 minutes. Add the garlic and sauté another minute. Add the beans, water, and sage sprig to the pot and bring slowly to a boil. Simmer, covered, for 2 hours, or until the beans are very tender. Remove the sage sprig.

While the beans are cooking, prepare the mushrooms and cook the tortellini. Soak the mushrooms in hot water to cover for 30 minutes. Remove the mushrooms, strain and reserve the soaking liquid, and gently rinse the mushrooms. Slice into thin strips and set aside with the soaking liquid. Add the mushrooms and soaking liquid to the beans about 30 minutes before they are done.

In a large pot, bring plenty of water to a gentle boil, add the pinch of salt, and cook the tortellini until just tender, 5 to 10 minutes. Home-made tortellini will cook faster than packaged fresh. Drain the tortellini and add it to the cooked beans. Season to taste with salt and freshly ground black pepper. Cook another 3 minutes, or long enough to reheat the tortellini if necessary. Just before serving, chop the reserved fennel leaves and sprinkle them on top. Serve with plenty of freshly grated pecorino on the side.

SERVES 6 to 8

1 pound dried Great Northern beans
2 fresh fennel bulbs, with tops
2 thick slices bacon, chopped
1 large onion, thinly sliced
2 garlic cloves, minced
6 cups water
1 sprig fresh sage
2 ounces dried porcini mushrooms (see Pantry)
Large pinch of salt
1 pound fresh cheese tortellini
Salt and freshly ground black pepper, to taste
Freshly grated pecorino cheese (see Pantry)

Opposite page: Pasta e Fagioli with White Beans, Tortellini, and Wild Mushrooms; top right: Risotto with Smoked Turkey, Mint, and Ricotta (recipe on page 38)

RISOTTO WITH SMOKED TURKEY, MINT, AND RICOTTA

Risotto is one of those very deceptive Italian dishes. While savoring its creamy, intricate flavor at a restaurant, it is easy to think that the dish would be impossible to create at home. In fact, risotto is Italian home cooking at its best: a bit time-consuming, yes, but satisfying to make; adaptable to the ingredients on hand and comforting to eat, but far from dull. You must use a plump, short-grain rice, such as Arborio, Superfino Arborio, or Roma rice imported from Italy. Use a heavy pot that will hold still on the stovetop, keep the broth hot the entire time you are cooking the risotto, and stir the rice almost constantly. For a creamy risotto, add a little liquid just at the end of cooking. To keep it stiff, stir the risotto until the excess liquid is absorbed. (RECIPE PHOTO ON PAGE 37, TOP RIGHT)

SERVES 4

6 cups chicken stock, low salt, defatted
4 tablespoons unsalted butter
2 tablespoons extra-virgin olive oil
1 small onion, finely chopped
2 cups Arborio rice (see Pantry)
½ cup dry white wine
4 ounces ricotta
¾ cup grated Parmesan cheese
1¼ cups shredded smoked turkey (approximately ¼ pound)
⅓ cup loosely packed fresh mint leaves, finely chopped
Salt and freshly ground black pepper, to taste

Heat the stock to a very low simmer. Keep hot throughout the cooking of the risotto.

Melt 2 tablespoons of the butter with the olive oil in a heavy saucepan over medium-low heat. When the butter foams, add the onion and sauté until wilted and golden, about 7 minutes. Add the rice and cook 2 minutes, stirring constantly, until it is well coated with butter and slightly opaque. Add the wine and stir constantly until all the wine is absorbed. Add the stock, one ladleful at a time, stirring frequently between each addition. Wait until nearly all the stock is absorbed before adding another ladleful.

Continue cooking the risotto in this way until the rice is just tender and the risotto is creamy and not stiff, 15 to 20 minutes. Remove from the heat.

Mix in the remaining 2 tablespoons of butter, the ricotta, and half of the Parmesan cheese. Add the turkey and mint. Season to taste with salt and pepper. Serve immediately, and pass the remaining Parmesan cheese.

BLACK BEAN CHILI CON CARNE WITH CILANTRO PESTO

SERVES 8 TO 10

2½ pounds boneless beef roast
4 tablespoons olive oil
½ pound ground pork
Salt, to taste
4 tablespoons ground mild red
  chilies or chili powder (see
  Pantry), or to taste
2 medium-sized red onions, thinly
  sliced
2 carrots, peeled and cut into 1½-
  inch julienne
2 celery stalks, cut into 1½-inch
  julienne
1 red bell pepper, seeded and cut
  into 1½-inch julienne
3 garlic cloves, minced
½ cup dry red wine
2 one-pound cans crushed
  tomatoes
2 cups water
4 tablespoons molasses
2 tablespoons chopped fresh sage,
  or 2 teaspoons dried sage
2½ teaspoons ground cumin
6 cups cooked black beans
Salt, to taste
Sour cream, for garnish
Cilantro Pesto (see recipe, page
  41)
Sour cream, for garnish
Chopped onion, for garnish
Grated cheese, for garnish
Chopped avocado, for garnish

Texans claim chili con carne as their own cowboy/caballero Tex-Mex creation, "a bowl of red" but with no beans. New Mexican varieties employ their distinctly earthy-tasting dried chilies. The truth, though, is that any large kettle of bubbling spicy sweet chili emits an aroma so enticing, so comforting, that almost no one can resist. This chili is yet another look at the possible combinations that can still be defined as chili, that wonderfully adaptable stew.

Slice the beef into very thin 2-inch strips. Heat 3 tablespoons of the olive oil in a large skillet over medium-high heat, and brown the beef in batches. Brown the ground pork. When all the meat is well browned, drain off any fat and put the meat back into the pan. Continue to brown for another few minutes until the meat is beginning to get crisp on the outside. Sprinkle with salt, add the chili powder, and allow it to cook for 1 minute, stirring constantly. Remove the skillet from the heat and set aside until needed.

In a large cast iron pot or casserole, heat the remaining 1 tablespoon of oil. Sauté the onions over medium heat until they begin to wilt, about 5 minutes. Add the carrots, celery, and red pepper and sauté 5 minutes more. Add the garlic and cook another minute. Lower the heat. Scrape the meat into the pot with the onion mixture. Heat the skillet again over medium-high heat and pour in the wine. Scrape up the browned bits and reduce the wine for a minute or so. Pour into the meat and vegetables.

Add the tomatoes, water, molasses, sage, and cumin to the pot. Simmer, covered, for 1½ hours, stirring occasionally. Add the black beans, drained of most of their liquid if canned, and season with salt if needed. Cook another 15 minutes. Put a dollop of Cilantro Pesto on each serving, and have sour cream, chopped onion, grated cheese, and avocado on the side.

(CONTINUED ON NEXT PAGE)

CILANTRO PESTO

3 bunches fresh cilantro (see
   Pantry), long stems removed
6 cloves garlic
6 tablespoons lime juice
½ cup olive oil
¾ cup sour cream
Salt, to taste

CILANTRO PESTO

Cilantro looks like a lacier version of Italian parsley, but its pungent citrus flavor is like nothing else. It may also be called coriander or Chinese parsley in the market.

Put the cilantro, garlic, and lime juice in the bowl of a food processor fitted with a steel blade. Process until the garlic and cilantro are finely minced (they can also be minced by hand). With the motor running, drizzle in the olive oil in a thin stream, or beat in by hand, until well incorporated. Scrape the pesto into a bowl and mix in the sour cream. Add salt to taste. Refrigerate until needed.

IRISH STEW WITH ROOT VEGETABLES AND STOUT

Irish stew is a classic example of "cottage cooking" at its finest—simple and delicious, satisfying, and unpretentious. Serve this dish with a loaf of grainy bread and a tall pint of stout.

Preheat the oven to 325°.

In a large skillet over low heat, cook the bacon until the fat is rendered, about 7 minutes. Remove the bacon and set aside. Dust the lamb pieces lightly with the flour and sprinkle with pepper. Working in batches, brown the lamb in the bacon fat over medium heat. Remove the browned lamb to a plate lined with paper towels and allow to drain. Pour the stout into the hot pan and scrape up the browned bits, reducing the liquid for 2 minutes. Turn off the heat.

In a large, ovenproof casserole with a tight-fitting lid, heat the olive oil. Sauté the leeks, parsnips, and carrots over medium heat until wilted, about 10 minutes. Turn off the heat.

Put the meat in with the vegetables and add the stout, broth, and thyme. Mix well. Spread the bread slice on one side with the mustard and place this on top, mustard side down.

Cover the casserole and cook in the preheated oven for 1½ hours. Stir well, mixing in the softened bread, and season to taste with salt and pepper. Sprinkle with chopped parsley and serve.

SERVES 6

4 slices thick bacon, diced
2½ pounds boneless lamb shoulder, cut into bite-sized pieces
4 tablespoons flour
Freshly ground black pepper
1 bottle (6 ounces) Irish stout
1½ tablespoons olive oil
3 large leeks, white part and 1 inch of green, sliced into ¼-inch rings
4 parsnips, peeled and cut into 1½-inch pieces
4 carrots, peeled and cut into 1½-inch pieces
2 cups beef broth, low salt
1 tablespoon fresh thyme leaves, or 1½ teaspoons dried thyme
1 large slice whole-grain bread
1 tablespoon Dijon mustard
Salt and freshly ground black pepper, to taste
Plenty of chopped fresh parsley

Opposite page, top left: Irish Stew with Root Vegetables and Stout; bottom right: Sausage, Parsnip, and Onion Pie (recipe on page 44)

SAUSAGE, PARSNIP, AND ONION PIE

Savory pies are a mainstay of British cooking, with the well-known steak and kidney pie at the apex. The sausages in this pie are far from the bangers of England; rather, they are chosen from the ever-expanding array of fresh gourmet sausages available in the American market. They mingle with woodsy sage, sweet parsnips, and little Italian onions. The sauce is light but rich and complex. To make the onions easier to peel, drop them in boiling water for 3 minutes. (RECIPE PHOTO ON PAGE 43, LOWER RIGHT)

Pile 1½ cups of the flour on a large wooden board or countertop, and add the pinch of salt. Cut 8 tablespoons (½ cup) of the butter into large chunks. With your fingertips, pinch the butter and flour together until the mixture resembles broken cornflakes. Scrape the mixture into a long rectangle, make a long ditch down the center, and put in 1 tablespoon of cold water. Lightly work the water and flour together until evenly moistened but not wet. Repeat this step with the other 3 tablespoons of water. Flatten the moistened dough with the heel of your hand. With a pastry scraper, scrape the dough back together and flatten any remaining nut-sized pieces. Gather the dough together into a ball and press it firmly into a 1-inch thick cake. Wrap it in plastic wrap and refrigerate until needed.

Peel the papery skins off the onions and trim off the root. In a large pot over low heat, melt 2 tablespoons of the butter. Sprinkle the onions with sugar and cook them, stirring often, until well browned, about 10 minutes. Remove to a plate lined with paper towels and allow to drain. Pour off the fat in the pot. In the same pot over medium heat, brown the sausage pieces. Remove and drain with the onions. Pour off any excess fat.

SERVES 4

1½ cups unbleached flour plus
  2 tablespoons
Pinch of salt
12 tablespoons unsalted cold
  butter
4 tablespoons ice-cold water
18 baby onions or cipollini (see
  Pantry), or 24 boiling onions
Small pinch of sugar
1 pound gourmet sausage,
  2 varieties, cut into bite-sized
  pieces
¼ cup red wine
2 medium-sized parsnips, peeled
  and cut into 1-inch pieces
1¼ cups beef broth
6 sage leaves, chopped, or
  1 teaspoon dried sage
8 parsley sprigs, chopped
Salt and freshly ground black
  pepper, to taste

Pour the wine into the pot, scraping up the brown bits from the bottom of the pot and cooking down the wine, about 2 minutes. Add the parsnips and broth and simmer, covered, until the parsnips are just tender, 15 minutes. Remove the parsnips with a slotted spoon and set aside with the onions and sausage.

Preheat the oven to 375°. With your fingers, mash the remaining 2 tablespoons of butter with the 2 tablespoons of flour until a paste forms. Break off a pinch of the butter-flour mixture and add it to the broth, stirring well to incorporate it. Continue to add pinches of the butter-flour mixture while cooking and stirring, until the broth is thickened, about 5 minutes. Turn off the heat. Add the sage and parsley, and season to taste with salt and pepper. Add the onions, sausage, and parsnips and mix well to coat all the pieces. Pour the mixture into a deep pie plate.

Remove the dough from the refrigerator and pinch off a chunk to use for making decorative shapes. Roll out the rest of the dough so that the circle is ½-inch larger all around than the pie plate. Lay the pastry over the pie plate, folding the excess edges under and crimping the edges all around. Press the edges firmly to the pie plate. Make several slits in the top. Roll out the extra dough, cut out desired shapes, and press them onto the top of the pie crust. Bake 35 to 45 minutes, until the crust is golden brown. Serve each slice with some of the sauce spooned on top.

SPRINGTIME VEGETABLE BORSCHT

Borscht is a fresh beet soup, a staple of Eastern Europe and Russia. Though the variations are limitless, borscht always contains beets and often beef. (Traditionally, beef was used to make the stock, but it was not served in the soup.) And no borscht would appear without its signature dollop of sour cream.

Heat the butter in a large soup pot. Sauté the leeks until wilted, about 5 minutes. Add the garlic and sauté another minute. Add the stock, beets, carrots, green beans, marjoram, caraway seeds, dill seed, bay leaf, and salt and simmer, covered, until everything is tender, about 35 minutes.

Remove the bay leaf and add salt and pepper to taste. Add the lemon juice and parsley and simmer another 10 minutes. Pour into bowls, and on each serving put a dollop of sour cream and a sprinkling of minced fresh chives.

SERVES 10

3 tablespoons butter
4 medium-sized leeks, white part only, halved, rinsed, and thinly sliced horizontally into 2-inch julienne strips
3 garlic cloves, minced to a paste
8 cups vegetable stock
1¼ pounds fresh beets, peeled and sliced into julienne strips
3 large carrots, peeled and sliced into julienne strips
¾ pound green beans, trimmed and sliced on a sharp diagonal into 1-inch ovals
1 tablespoon chopped fresh marjoram leaves, or 1 teaspoon dried marjoram
½ teaspoon caraway seeds
½ teaspoon dill seed
1 bay leaf
¾ teaspoon salt
Freshly ground black pepper, to taste
3 tablespoons lemon juice
2 tablespoons chopped fresh parsley
Sour cream
Minced fresh chives

SUKIYAKI

In Japan, sukiyaki falls under the general category of nabemono, or food "cooked at the table." This well-known dish is typically a winter meal—a cozy gathering around a hot iron pot in which the world's best beef and the freshest vegetables simmer lightly.

Sukiyaki has an interesting history. Beef was not eaten in Japan until relatively recently, since Buddhist belief prohibited it. In the mid-19th century when the Japanese came in contact with a large number of Europeans, they observed that the Westerners were larger in stature and surmised that their meat-inclusive diet was responsible. In 1872 the Emperor of Japan declared that, in the best interest of the Empire, he, himself, would eat beef. This opened the door for the creation of all sorts of new dishes. The name sukiyaki comes from the Japanese for "grilled on a plow blade," suggesting either that the farmers who first created the dish cooked the meat on the blade of a plow, so as not to break the religious taboo of using kitchen cookware for meat, or that, simply, the meat was cooked fresh and fast, grilled right over a hot fire. In either case, sukiyaki has evolved over time into a fashionable and luxurious meal, with specific and ritualized preparation and presentation. In Japan the dish is very expensive because of the high cost of beef, and entire restaurants are devoted to serving sukiyaki.

To make sukiyaki at home, you can use a small tabletop burner and a cast iron pot. The traditional sukiyaki pot is either decorative cast iron or earthenware. Sukiyaki can also be made in one or two electric skillets, or in the kitchen on the stove, if necessary. It is delicious served with bowls of rice for each person, but according to Japanese tradition, if sake is served with the sukiyaki, the rice should be held off until later! Have all the ingredients for the sukiyaki attractively arranged on platters—part of the charm of the presentation is in the beauty of the raw ingredients before they go into the broth.

Ask the butcher to slice the meat paper thin, or freeze it for an hour before slicing it yourself. Sukiyaki is traditionally served with a beaten raw egg, seasoned with a drop or two of soy sauce, into which each diner dips the piping hot meat and vegetables. In view of current concerns about eating uncooked egg, this part of the meal can be omitted.

Mix the mirin, sake, soy sauce, stock, and sugar together in a small pitcher to make the sauce. Set aside until needed.

Slice the beef across the grain into paper-thin slices. Divide the slices and arrange on two platters. Divide the onion wedges and carrots between the platters. Wipe the shiitakes clean with a damp paper towel (do not run under water). Cut each shiitake cap into 4 slices. Cut the tofu loaf into ¾-inch slices, and cut these rectangles into triangular wedges. Place them on the platters. Slice the green onion tops into fourths (to make a "fringed" top). Place these and the noodles on the platters. Cover and refrigerate one of the platters until needed.

If you are serving the egg dip, have four dipping bowls ready, with a beaten egg in each. A dash of soy sauce may be added to the beaten egg, if desired. Have rice ready in individual bowls and chopsticks for each diner.

SERVES 4

½ cup mirin (see Pantry)
½ cup sake (see Pantry)
½ cup soy sauce
1½ cups chicken stock, low salt, defatted
2 tablespoons sugar
¾ pound best-quality boneless beef, from the rib or loin
1 large yellow onion, peeled and sliced into wedges
2 medium carrots, peeled and thinly sliced on the diagonal
8 fresh shiitake mushrooms (see Pantry), stems removed
½ pound firm tofu
8 green onions, white part and half the green tops, roots trimmed off
½ pound shirataki noodles (see Pantry), drained
4 eggs, beaten (optional)
6 cups cooked short-grain rice
4 tablespoons vegetable oil

Have the first platter at hand, with a pair of chopsticks for turning the ingredients. Heat half the oil in the cast iron pot over medium-high heat. Brown the beef slices quickly on both sides, cooking in batches and taking care not to overlap. Remove the slices to a plate. Add the yellow onion and the carrots to the pot and cook for about 2 minutes. Add the mushrooms, browning them a little. You can move the other ingredients to the side to make this easier. Add the tofu, and allow it to sear and brown lightly on two sides. Turn it carefully to keep it from breaking apart. Add the green onions, and sear them lightly. Searing the vegetables and tofu should altogether take no more than 5 minutes. Pour half the sauce into the pot. Make space for the noodles on one side of the pot and add them, and add the browned beef. Simmer the sauce for another 3 minutes or so. While the sauce is simmering, gently turn and poke and adjust the vegetables and meat so that everything cooks evenly.

Each person can serve him- or herself from the pot, picking out pieces and bringing them to the rice bowl. Ladle some of the broth over the rice as well. When the first batch of sukiyaki has been eaten and all the broth consumed, wipe the pot dry and prepare another batch with the other half of the ingredients.

KEDGEREE

This delicious breakfast dish represents one of the great British interpretations of Indian cuisine. It is based on the East Indian khichri, a dish of rice and onions. When the British absorbed it during their long colonization of India, they added smoked fish and egg, already favorite English staples. To acknowledge its mixed origins, serve kedgeree with a variety of chutneys and freshly baked scones.

Check the fish for bones, and use tweezers to remove any you find. Place the fish in a large pot and add the milk, parsley, salt, and peppercorns. Bring to a gentle boil, reduce the heat to a simmer, and poach the fish, covered, until it begins to flake, about 10 minutes. Remove with a slotted spoon and drain on paper towels. Strain and reserve the poaching liquid. When the fish is cool enough to handle, remove the skin and discard it, and break the fish into large flakes. Set aside until needed.

In a large casserole with a tight-fitting lid, melt the butter over medium heat and cook the onion until browning, about 10 minutes. Add the rice, curry, cardamom seeds, cayenne, and nutmeg and sauté until the rice turns opaque, about 5 minutes.

Add the poaching liquid, the bay leaf, and enough water to come ½ inch above the surface of the rice. Bring to a boil over high heat and continue to boil, uncovered, until the surface of the rice looks pitted and bubbly, and some of the liquid has been absorbed, about 10 minutes. Cover and reduce the heat to low. Cook another 10 minutes, or until the rice is tender and dry. Remove and discard the bay leaf.

Over low heat, gently mix in the flaked fish, the cream or half-and-half, eggs, raisins, green onions, and parsley. Season to taste with salt and pepper. Heat through, but do not cook. The kedgeree should be firm and a little moist.

SERVES 6

¾ pound smoked cod or haddock
1 cup milk
3 parsley sprigs
Pinch of salt
6 peppercorns
4 tablespoons unsalted butter
1 small onion, thinly sliced
2¼ cups long-grain rice
3 tablespoons curry powder
Seeds from 8 cardamom pods
Cayenne pepper, to taste
Pinch of ground nutmeg
1 bay leaf
1 cup heavy cream or half-and-half
4 hard-boiled eggs, chopped
½ cup raisins
6 green onions, white part and half the green, minced
⅓ cup Italian parsley, chopped
Salt and freshly ground black pepper, to taste

CIOPPINO

According to culinary legend, this hearty and delicious seafood stew was created by San Francisco's Italian community in the North Beach part of the city and is a true North Beach dish. While every coastal Italian town has its own zuppa di pesce, *this particular dish is uniquely San Franciscan by virtue of the Dungeness crab. Serve this stew with lots of great bread for soaking up the flavorful sauce.*

In a large heavy casserole, heat the olive oil over medium heat and sauté the onion and carrots until soft and browning, about 10 minutes. Add the garlic and sauté another minute. Add the wine, tomatoes, water, tomato paste, oregano, thyme, dried red pepper, and salt and mix well. Simmer, covered, for 45 minutes. Adjust the seasonings.

While the soup is cooking, twist off the crab legs and crack the shells in various places. Remove the meat from the body. Set the meat and crab legs aside until needed.

Add the clams to the cooked sauce and simmer, covered, for 5 minutes. Add the fish and simmer another 3 minutes. Add the crab meat, crab legs, and shrimp and simmer until the crab is heated through and the shrimp has lost its translucency. Discard any clams that do not open.

Ladle the stew into large heated bowls and serve with a pinch of chopped basil and parsley on top.

SERVES 6

¼ cup olive oil
1 onion, minced
2 carrots, peeled and minced
2 garlic cloves, minced
1 cup red wine
5 large tomatoes, peeled and chopped
3 cups water
2 tablespoons tomato paste
1 tablespoon chopped fresh oregano, or 1 teaspoon dried oregano
1 tablespoon fresh thyme leaves, or 1 teaspoon dried thyme
½ teaspoon minced dried red chili pepper, or to taste
Salt, to taste
1 medium-sized Dungeness crab, cooked and cleaned
18 cherrystone clams, thoroughly scrubbed
1 pound firm white fish fillets, boned and cut into chunks
¾ pound medium-sized raw shrimp, shelled and deveined
Fresh basil leaves, chopped
Italian parsley, chopped

KATSUDON WITH SHIITAKE MUSHROOMS

Tonkatsu, *breaded and deep-fried pork cutlet, is a dish as common in Japan as the hamburger is in America. And* katsudon, *one of the tonkatsu variations, is a delicious meal-in-a-bowl (a* donburi*) made of pork cutlet,* katsu, *over rice. Tonkatsu is somewhat of a culinary departure from most Japanese cuisine. It is a more straight-forward meat dish, breaded and fried, unlike the light tempura bat-ter fries. But pork was brought to Japan only in the last century, and its preparation has a distinctly European style. It is almost exclusive-ly deep-fried, but the result is flavorful and light, unlike some fried foods of Western origin. This katsudon adds the earthy, smoky flavor of shiitake mushrooms to round out the savory pork and its sweet sauce.*

Place the rice in a colander or strainer and rinse under running water for several minutes, until the water is clear. Place in a deep pot and add enough water to come 1 inch above the surface of the rice. Bring the water to a boil and cook uncovered, over medium-high heat, until the water is even with the top of the rice, about 7 minutes. Reduce the heat to very low, cover, and cook the rice until it is tender and the water absorbed, about 20 minutes. Do not open the pot while the rice is cooking.

Pour the boiling water over the dried mushrooms and soak them while you prepare the cutlets.

Flatten the cutlets slightly with a smooth meat pounder. Sprinkle with salt and pepper. In a bowl, beat 2 of the eggs. Dust the cutlets with flour, dip in the beaten egg, and immediately dip in the bread crumbs, coating all sides thickly and evenly.

Heat ½ inch of oil in a skillet to 350°, or use a deep fryer. Fry the cutlets, one at a time, until golden brown, about 4 minutes per side. Remove to drain on a dish lined with paper towels. When all the cutlets are cooked, slice each one crosswise into ½-inch slices. Keep warm in a low oven.

(CONTINUED ON NEXT PAGE)

SERVES 4

2½ cups short-grain rice
1 cup boiling water
4 to 6 dried shiitake mushrooms
   (see Pantry), depending on size
4 boneless pork cutlets, ½- to ¾-
   inch thick, from the tenderloin
   or loin (about ¼ pound each)
Salt and freshly ground black
   pepper
6 eggs
Flour
1 cup fresh bread crumbs
Vegetable oil
1 onion, thinly sliced
1 cup chicken stock, low salt,
   defatted
½ cup mirin (see Pantry)
⅔ cup soy sauce
4 green onions, white part and
   half the green leaves, sliced
   diagonally into 1-inch pieces

Opposite page, lower left: Katsudon with Shiitake Mushrooms; top right: Chinese Sandpot with Spicy Meatballs and Black Mushrooms (recipe on page 59)

In a bowl, beat the remaining 4 eggs, and set aside until needed. Heat ½ tablespoon of oil in a large skillet over medium heat. Sauté the onion until wilted, about 5 minutes. Pour the mushroom soaking liquid in with the onions, taking care not to pour in any grit that may have accumulated on the bottom. Thinly slice the mushrooms and add them to the onions. Add the chicken stock, mirin, and soy sauce and reduce the heat. Simmer for 1 minute. Add the green onion and simmer 2 more minutes. Pour the beaten eggs carefully over the simmering sauce. When the eggs begin to set, push them gently with a spoon to redistribute and cook evenly. The eggs are not blended into but cooked on top of the sauce, in ribbons. Cook the eggs until they have lost their translucent look but are still soft. They should not be dry and hard.

To assemble the dish, divide the rice among 4 deep bowls. Arrange the sliced pork cutlets over the rice. Using a large spoon, spoon the onion, mushroom, and egg sauce over the top of the rice and cutlets. Serve immediately.

CHINESE SANDPOT WITH SPICY MEATBALLS
AND BLACK MUSHROOMS

SERVES 4

MUSHROOM STOCK

4 cups chicken stock, low salt,
  defatted
1½ tablespoons soy sauce
2 tablespoons Chinese rice wine
  (see Pantry), or dry sherry
½ teaspoon sugar
2 whole star anise (see Pantry)
½ teaspoon minced dried red
  chilies (see Pantry)
2 green onions, white part and
  half the green, thinly sliced
8 dried Chinese black mushrooms
  (see Pantry)

MEATBALLS

1 pound ground pork
2 garlic cloves, minced to a paste
2 green onions, white part and
  half the green, finely minced
½ inch piece ginger, peeled and
  finely minced
1 small green chili, such as
  serrano (see Pantry), finely
  minced
1 tablespoon finely grated orange
  rind
1 tablespoon soy sauce
1 tablespoon Chinese rice wine
  (see Pantry), or dry sherry
¼ teaspoon sugar
¼ teaspoon salt

*A*lthough we most often associate Chinese cuisine with quickly cooked stir-fried dishes that are served over rice, stewing has a long tradition in Chinese cookery. In Beijing there is a restaurant called Shaguoju (meaning, roughly, "sandpot bureau"), said to be the first restaurant in that city. It originated in the mid-18th century, in the guardhouse of an Imperial palace—the result of quick-thinking, entrepreneurial impulses. The palace's resident aristocrat, like others of his ilk, made a large, showy offering one religious holiday, sacrificing hundreds of whole pigs on that single day. The excess meat was given to the palace eunuchs and guards, who, in their thriftiness, created individual stewed pots and sold them to the public. This custom established the site as a true restaurant, which still carries on the same traditions and serves the same specialty in sandpot dishes. (RECIPE PHOTO ON PAGE 57, TOP RIGHT)

MUSHROOM STOCK

Heat the chicken stock. Pour the hot stock into a bowl with the soy sauce, rice wine, sugar, star anise, chilies, green onions, and dried mushrooms. Allow the mushrooms to soak for 30 minutes, then remove them from the stock. Discard the stems, and slice the mushrooms into ½-inch strips. Reserve the mushrooms. Remove the star anise and reserve the stock until needed.

MEATBALLS

In a bowl, mix together the pork, garlic, green onions, ginger, chili, orange rind, soy sauce, rice wine, sugar, and salt until well blended. Using your hands, shape the meat into balls about the size of a walnut and set aside on a plate.

(CONTINUED ON NEXT PAGE)

SANDPOT STEW

In a wok or large skillet, heat the oil over high heat. Add the ginger, garlic, and black beans to the wok, and sizzle for 5 seconds. Add the onion and carrot and cook another minute. Add the cabbage and toss for a minute; add ⅓ cup of the stock and stir-fry until the cabbage is wilted, about 3 minutes.

Put the contents of the wok into a 2- to 3-quart sandpot or casserole. Arrange the meatballs and sliced mushrooms on top of the vegetables, and pour the remaining stock over the top. Put the cilantro sprigs on top. Cover and bring to a boil very slowly over medium-low heat. Reduce the heat and simmer over low heat for 40 minutes.

SANDPOT STEW

1 tablespoon peanut or vegetable oil

½-inch piece ginger, peeled and minced

1 garlic clove, minced

1 tablespoon finely chopped Chinese black beans (see Pantry)

½ small onion, halved and thinly sliced

1 large carrot, peeled and sliced into 2-inch julienne strips

1 small Napa cabbage head, halved, cored, and sliced lengthwise into ribbons

2 or 3 fresh cilantro sprigs

BLANQUETTE OF VEAL WITH FENNEL

SERVES 6

2 fennel bulbs
1 tablespoon olive oil
1 onion, halved and sliced
2 cups chicken stock, low salt, defatted
1½ cups water
2½ pounds boneless veal breast or shoulder, cut into bite-sized pieces
1 garlic clove, slightly crushed
1 bay leaf
2 fresh thyme sprigs
3 fresh Italian parsley sprigs
2 fresh tarragon sprigs
Salt and freshly ground white pepper
4 tablespoons butter
4 tablespoons flour
2 egg yolks
1 tablespoon lemon juice
⅓ cup cream

Though it is tempting to think of this stew as being "blanketed" by a creamy white sauce, blanquette comes from the French word blanc, *for white, referring to its light color. It is usually made from lighter meat—chicken or veal—simmered in broth or water, with cream and egg added at the end. The meat is not browned at all, to prevent marring the perfect off-white color of the dish. In this dish the onion and fennel are sautéed together to bring out their sweetness and flavor before they are simmered with the veal.*

Slice the feathery green tops off the fennel bulbs and reserve some of the little green leaves. Halve the bulbs, pull off and discard any brown or tough-looking layers, cut out the hard core, and slice the fennel lengthwise into thick strips. Heat the oil in a large, heavy casserole over medium heat. Sauté the fennel and onion until just wilted, about 5 minutes. Scrape into a bowl and set aside.

In the same casserole put the chicken stock, water, and veal. Slowly bring the stock to a low boil, skimming off any foam that rises to the top. When the stock is mostly clear, add the fennel and onions, garlic clove, and bay leaf. Tie the thyme, parsley, and tarragon sprigs together and add them to the pot. Season with salt and pepper. Cook, covered, over low heat for 1½ hours, or until the veal is quite tender.

With a slotted spoon, remove the veal, fennel, and onions to a dish and keep warm. Remove and discard the garlic clove, bay leaf, and herb sprigs. Strain the stock through several layers of cheesecloth and put it back into the pot. Keep it hot on the stove.

In a small saucepan, melt the butter over low heat and add the flour. Whisking constantly, cook the butter and flour until foaming, about 2 minutes. Whisk in a ladleful of the hot veal stock, and then whisk this back into the stock. Simmer the stock, uncovered, for 5 minutes, until thickened and smooth. Add salt and pepper to taste.

(CONTINUED ON NEXT PAGE)

Whisk the egg yolks, lemon juice, and cream together in a small bowl. Whisk in a ladleful of the thickened sauce, and then whisk this back into the pot. Cook over low heat, whisking constantly, until smooth. Do not boil the sauce. Add the veal and fennel, and keep over very low heat for another 10 minutes to meld the flavors. Chop the reserved fennel leaves, sprinkle on the stew, and serve.

COUSCOUS WITH CHICKEN, BUTTERNUT SQUASH, AND FAVA BEANS

Couscous is said to be the national dish of Morocco, although it ranks almost as highly in the cuisines of Algeria and Tunisia. When the Arab world controlled Spain in the Middle Ages, couscous was brought into the region and became a staple of the diet. But when the Muslims were expelled from Spain, all obvious culinary influences were cast out as well, and couscous became a "dish non grata," even banned by the Spanish Inquisition! It was subsequently nearly forgotten in Europe and has only in this century reappeared in the cafés of Paris, thanks to entrepreneurial North African immigrants.

Couscous is made of semolina grain that has been ground, moistened, and rolled into tiny pellets. Couscous also refers to the entire dish, consisting of a flavorful stew, or tajine, served over steamed couscous grains. Traditionally a couscoussier (a two-level cooking pot with a deep bottom half and perforated top half) is used, with the stew simmering in the bottom and the couscous steaming in the top. Most couscous available in our markets is precooked and needs only to be steeped in some of the stew liquid for several minutes and fluffed.

Soak the beans overnight in plenty of cold water, or use the quick-soak method: bring the beans and water to a rolling boil, remove from heat, and let stand, covered, for 1 hour.

Drain the beans and put them in a large casserole with plenty of water. Stud the whole onion with the cloves, and put it in the pot. Bring the beans to a boil, reduce the heat, and simmer, covered, for 45 minutes. Drain the beans and discard the onion.

Meanwhile, heat the oil over medium heat in the bottom of a couscoussier or large casserole. Thoroughly brown the chicken pieces in batches until golden, remove them to paper towels, and allow to drain. When all the chicken is browned, pour off all but a tablespoon or so of oil. Sauté the sliced onion until browning, about 10 minutes. Add the garlic, coriander, cumin, ginger, turmeric, and plenty of salt and pepper and sauté another 1 minute. Return the browned chicken to the pot and add the beans, chicken stock, water, butternut squash, potatoes, carrots, bay leaf, and cinnamon stick. Bring to a boil. Reduce the heat and simmer, covered, for 1 hour. Adjust the seasonings and add the raisins.

Meanwhile, 10 minutes before the stew has finished cooking, prepare the couscous. Line the top section of the couscoussier with cheesecloth and place the dry couscous in it. Using a ladle, dip out 4 cups of the cooking liquid from the stew. Place the top section onto the bottom section, pour the cooking liquid over the couscous, cover, and let it steam over the stew.

SERVES 8

¾ pound dried fava beans (see Pantry), washed and picked over
3 large onions, 1 whole, 2 halved and thinly sliced
8 whole cloves
4 tablespoons olive oil
1 chicken, 3 to 4 pounds, cut up
6 garlic cloves, minced to a paste
2 teaspoons ground coriander
½ teaspoon ground cumin
2 teaspoons ground ginger
½ teaspoon turmeric
Salt and freshly ground black pepper, to taste
4 cups chicken stock, low salt, defatted
4 cups water
1 butternut squash, about 2 pounds, peeled, seeded, and sliced into 1-inch pieces
2 large potatoes, peeled and sliced into 1-inch pieces
2 carrots, peeled and coarsely chopped
1 bay leaf
1 cinnamon stick
½ cup golden raisins
3 cups (20 ounces) couscous (see Pantry)
Chopped cilantro
Harissa (see Pantry)

If you are not using a couscoussier, dip out 4¼ cups of the cooking liquid and put it into a saucepan. Bring it to a boil, pour in the couscous, and stir. Turn off the heat, cover, and allow the couscous to stand for 7 minutes.

Before serving, fluff the couscous with a fork, and pile it in a pyramid on a large platter. Make a well in the top. Arrange the chicken pieces around the edge of the platter, and spoon some of the stew into the well. Sprinkle with cilantro and serve with harissa on the side, so that each diner can spice up his or her own stew. The additional stew can also be served on the side.

PASTEL DE PAPA

*A*rgentina is a vast country of acres and acres of cattle-grazing lands. Because of the high beef production, beef is central to the country's cuisine. This "potato pie," an Argentine shepherd's pie made with ground beef, is a cozy, filling meal to have with a sturdy red wine or beer and a salad of mixed sweet and tangy greens.

Preheat the oven to 375°.

Bring a large pot of water to a rolling boil. Add the salt, then add the potatoes and garlic. Reduce the heat and cook the potatoes until very tender. Drain the potatoes and garlic, and put them in the bowl of a mixer. Add the butter, milk, and sour cream and whip at medium speed until the potatoes are light and smooth. They should be a little wet. Season to taste with salt and pepper.

While the potatoes are cooking, heat the olive oil in a large skillet and cook the onions and pepper until wilted and browning, about 10 minutes. Scrape them onto a plate and set aside. Brown the ground beef in the same pan until well cooked. Pour off the excess fat. To the ground beef add the cooked onions and pepper, the tomatoes, raisins, and olives, and cook another 10 minutes. Season to taste with salt and pepper.

In the bottom of a deep, buttered earthenware pot or baking dish, spread ¼ of the potato mixture. Put the meat mixture on this, arrange the hard-boiled eggs on top of the meat, then put the remaining potatoes on top.

Bake for 35 to 40 minutes, or until the potatoes are nicely browned on top.

SERVES 8

Large pinch of salt
5 large Idaho potatoes, peeled
20 garlic cloves, peeled and root ends trimmed
3 tablespoons butter
⅓ cup milk
½ cup sour cream or plain yogurt
Salt and freshly ground black pepper, to taste
2 tablespoons olive oil
2 large red onions, halved and thinly sliced
1 red bell pepper, seeded and thinly sliced
1¾ pounds lean ground beef
2 large tomatoes, seeded and chopped
⅔ cup black raisins
12 green olives, pitted and chopped
3 hard-boiled eggs, peeled and sliced

THAI GREEN SHRIMP CURRY

Of the three colorful Thai curries—green, red, and yellow—green is the hottest. It is widely loved and highly regarded, and is often served at special occasions. The flavor of lemongrass, an essential ingredient in Thai cooking, gives a citrus sweetness to balance the heat of the chilies. Adjust the heat of the curry by adding more chilies to the paste, by using more of the curry paste in the coconut sauce, or by adding sliced chilies to the sauce before serving. Serve this delicious dish with the rice used in Thailand: an aromatic long-grain rice with the sweet smell of jasmine.

To make the Green Curry Paste, put all the ingredients in a food processor or blender and process thoroughly to make a smooth paste. This paste will keep in the refrigerator for several weeks in a jar with a tight-fitting top, or it can be frozen indefinitely.

In a saucepan, bring the thick coconut milk to a gentle boil. Simmer and stir until oily and thickened, 6 to 8 minutes. Add the curry paste and cook, stirring constantly, until fragrant, another 2 minutes. Add the thin coconut milk, *nam pla,* eggplant, and sugar and simmer, uncovered, for 10 minutes. Add the shrimp, bell peppers, 16 of the basil leaves, and Thai chilies and simmer another 5 minutes. Serve immediately with steamed rice, and sprinkle the reserved basil leaves on top.

SERVES 6

GREEN CURRY

2 cups thick coconut milk (see Pantry)

½ to ⅔ cup Green Curry Paste (see recipe)

4 cups thin coconut milk (see Pantry)

2 tablespoons *nam pla* (see Pantry)

6 small Thai eggplants (see Pantry), or Japanese eggplants, diced

½ teaspoon sugar

36 large shrimp (approximately 1½ pounds), shelled and deveined

½ red bell pepper, sliced into julienne strips

½ green bell pepper, sliced into julienne strips

22 whole small basil leaves

2 fresh green or red Thai chilies, or *serranos* (see Pantry), stemmed and sliced into ovals, optional

GREEN CURRY PASTE

8 to 12 fresh green Thai chilies, or serranos (see Pantry), stemmed and coarsely chopped

3 stalks fresh lemongrass (see Pantry), using 2 inches above the root, chopped

1-inch piece fresh galangal (see Pantry), peeled, sliced, and coarsely chopped

4 whole fresh or frozen kaffir lime leaves (see Pantry), rib removed, chopped

1 teaspoon finely grated kaffir lime rind

1 bunch fresh cilantro (see Pantry), including roots, stems, and leaves

2 garlic cloves, halved

4 shallots, quartered

1 teaspoon ground coriander

½ teaspoon ground cumin

½ teaspoon turmeric

1 tablespoon *nam pla* (see Pantry)

2 teaspoons sugar

1 teaspoon *kapi* (see Pantry)

CORNED BEEF AND CABBAGE

Corned beef and cabbage, a dish usually reserved for Saint Patrick's Day, is too easy and delicious to be relegated to that once-a-year slot. Its near relative, the New England boiled dinner, has always been a classic American meal of the hearty sort. Serve it to a big rollicking crowd with lots of good mustards, horseradish cream sauce, and fresh hot cornbread (wonderful with butter and molasses). Corned beef often comes with spices provided. Adjust the amount of spices you use depending on what is included with the corned beef.

In a large kettle or pot, place the brisket and its juices and seasonings, if included. Coarsely chop one onion and one carrot. Add the chopped carrot and onion, the vinegar, stout, mustard, peppercorns, coriander, caraway, fennel seeds, sage, and bay leaves. Add water to barely cover, and bring to a boil. Reduce the heat, cover, and simmer for 2½ to 3 hours, until the meat is tender when pierced with a fork.

Slice the remaining onions into wedges, and peel and slice the remaining carrots into chunks. Slice the cabbage heads in half, cut out the cores, and slice each cabbage half into 3 wedges (for 12 wedges). Add the onions, carrots, and potatoes to the broth. Arrange the cabbage wedges carefully on top. Cover and simmer another 45 minutes, or until all the vegetables are tender.

Carefully remove the corned beef to a carving board, taking care to keep the cabbage wedges intact. Trim off any excess fat. Slice across the grain and arrange the meat in the middle of a large platter. Arrange the cabbage wedges and other vegetables around the meat, and ladle some of the broth over everything. Sprinkle with chopped parsley and serve with mustards, Horseradish Cream Sauce, and broth on the side.

HORSERADISH CREAM SAUCE

Beat the cream until it forms soft peaks. Gently fold in the horseradish and mustard. Season to taste with salt and pepper and refrigerate until needed.

SERVES 10 TO 12

6-pound corned beef brisket
5 onions
7 carrots
½ cup malt vinegar
1 bottle (6 ounces) Irish stout
2 tablespoons course-grain mustard
10 black peppercorns
1 tablespoon coriander seeds
1 tablespoon caraway seeds
1 tablespoon fennel seeds
Several sprigs fresh sage, or 1 tablespoon dried sage
2 bay leaves
2 heads green cabbage
24 small new red potatoes
3 tablespoons chopped fresh Italian parsley
A choice of different mustards Horseradish Cream Sauce (see recipe, below)

HORSERADISH CREAM SAUCE

¾ cup heavy or whipping cream
4 tablespoons prepared horseradish, drained
1 tablespoon Dijon mustard
Salt and freshly ground black pepper, to taste

Opposite page, top left: Corned Beef and Cabbage; lower right: Ham, Turnip and Apple Pie with a Cornbread Crust (recipe on page 74)

HAM, TURNIP, AND APPLE PIE WITH A CORNBREAD CRUST

*T*his twist on all-American ingredients puts savory and sweet
together, baked with the cornbread right on the top. The United
States has an inventive casserole tradition that boomed in the 1940s
and 1950s, and although the children of that generation sometimes
look down on the casserole, there is often no substitute for a hearty
one-dish meal, with the bread baked right in. (RECIPE PHOTO ON PAGE 73,
LOWER RIGHT)

Heat 1 tablespoon of the olive oil in a large skillet over medium heat.
Sauté the onion until wilted, about 5 minutes. Add the turnips and apples
and sauté another 5 minutes. Add the caraway seeds, mix well, and scrape the
mixture into a bowl. Set aside until needed.

In the same skillet, heat the remaining 1 tablespoon of olive oil and the
butter. Sauté the ham over medium heat until lightly browned, about 5 minutes. Remove the ham with a slotted spoon and set aside until needed. Pour
off all but 3 tablespoons of fat, or add butter if needed. Reduce the heat to
low and sprinkle in the flour. Whisking constantly, cook the flour until it is a
nut-brown color, about 3 minutes. Whisk in the chicken stock and cook
until the sauce is thick and smooth, another 3 minutes. Season to taste.

Mix the ham, onions, turnips, apples, and parsley into the sauce. Cook 3
minutes, mixing well. Keep over low heat while you prepare the cornbread.

Spread the cornbread batter evenly over the ham mixture in the pie dish.
Bake the pie in the oven for 35 to 40 minutes, until the top of the cornbread
is nicely browned.

CORNBREAD CRUST
Preheat the oven to 350°. Thoroughly combine the cornmeal, flour, brown
sugar, baking powder, baking soda, and salt in a large bowl. In a measuring
cup, beat the egg, milk, and melted butter together. Stir this into the dry
mixture and blend well. The batter should be thick and spreadable, not
pourable.

SERVES 6

2 tablespoons olive oil
1 large red onion, halved and
  sliced
2 medium-sized turnips, peeled
  and diced
2 green apples, cored and diced
1 teaspoon caraway seeds
1 tablespoon butter
1¼ pounds smoked ham, such
  as Black Forest, diced
2 tablespoons flour
1 cup chicken stock, low salt,
  defatted
Salt and freshly ground black
  pepper, to taste
1 heaping tablespoon chopped
  fresh parsley
Cornbread Crust (see recipe)

CORNBREAD CRUST
1⅓ cups cornmeal
¾ cup unbleached flour
2 tablespoons brown sugar
2 teaspoons baking powder
1 teaspoon baking soda
¼ teaspoon salt
1 egg
¾ cup milk
2 tablespoons melted butter

COQ AU VIN WITH ROASTED BABY VEGETABLES

SERVES 6

1 large chicken, about 4 pounds,
  cut into 8 pieces
1 bottle red Burgundy wine
10 black peppercorns
Salt and freshly ground black
  pepper
Flour
4 slices thick bacon, about 3
  ounces, diced
3 garlic cloves, slightly crushed
4 sprigs fresh thyme
4 sprigs fresh Italian parsley
1 sprig fresh rosemary
1 bay leaf
24 small mushrooms
24 cipollini (see Pantry), or
  little onions
24 baby carrots
24 baby zucchini
3 tablespoons olive oil
2 teaspoons chopped fresh
  rosemary
1½ tablespoons butter
1½ tablespoons flour
Chopped fresh parsley, for garnish

This delicious dish from the Burgundy region of France began as a humble midday meal for vineyard workers and employed the very wine they toiled for. Traditionally the coq in this dish is a more mature and larger cockerel or rooster, or sometimes a capon, which benefits from a marinade and long braising. For this recipe one large chicken serves very well, and it does not require such a long time in the pot. Use a good-quality dry red wine from Burgundy to experience the authentic flavor of this hearty stew, and then drink a second bottle with the meal.

Place the chicken in a glass or pottery bowl with the wine and peppercorns. Marinate 1 to 2 hours in the refrigerator.

Remove the chicken from the marinade and reserve the marinade. Pat the chicken dry. Season the pieces with salt and pepper, dust lightly with flour, and set aside until needed.

In a large, heavy casserole, cook the bacon until golden and the fat is rendered, about 7 minutes. Do not let it get crisp. Remove the bacon with a slotted spoon and reserve. In the same pot over medium heat, brown the chicken in batches and remove to drain. Discard the fat in the pot. Pour in the reserved marinade, scraping up all the browned bits on the bottom of the pot. Bring it to a boil. Reduce the heat and put the chicken, garlic, and cooked bacon in the pot. Tie the thyme, parsley, rosemary, and bay leaf together in a bundle, and add this to the pot. Cover with the lid slightly askew and simmer for 1 hour.

While the chicken is cooking, prepare the vegetables. Preheat the oven to 425°. Clean the mushrooms by brushing off the dirt with a dry paper towel or a mushroom brush. Trim the root end and peel the skins off the onions. Remove the green tops from the carrots, wash the carrots and zucchini, and pat them dry. Put all the vegetables in a large bowl, drizzle with olive oil and sprinkle with rosemary, and toss well to coat each vegetable. Arrange the vegetables on a large baking sheet and sprinkle with salt and pepper. Roast the vegetables until golden brown and tender when pierced with a skewer, about 45 minutes, turning them once during cooking. Keep warm until needed. (CONTINUED ON NEXT PAGE)

When the chicken is done, remove it to a deep platter and keep it warm. Remove and discard the garlic cloves and the herb bundle. Spoon off some of the fat from the top of the sauce. With your fingers, mash the butter and flour together and add this to the sauce, bit by bit and whisking all the while. Cook the sauce until it has thickened, about 5 minutes.

Arrange the roasted vegetables around the chicken. Generously spoon the sauce over the chicken, and drizzle some on the vegetables. Sprinkle the chicken with chopped fresh parsley. Serve immediately with the remaining sauce on the side.

CASSOULET WITH DUCK, LAMB, AND GARLIC SAUSAGE

*T*hree cities vie for credit for having created the ultimate and original *cassoulet: Toulouse, Castelnaudary, and Carcassonne, all in the Languedoc region of France. Each town's version uses slightly different meats, and as a result, this embattled triumvirate agrees only on the use of the small dried white haricot (or navy) bean. Another point of contention has to do with the number of times the crust is broken and stirred back into the stew; according to one city it should be seven times, while another argues for eight. Fresh duck is used in this recipe, although traditionally cassoulet is made with goose or duck confit, the bird cooked and preserved in its own fat. The dish is named for the pot in which it is cooked, a cassole, which is a deep earthenware casserole the looks of which would be enough to convince you that its contents will be appetizing.*

Drain and rinse the soaked beans and pick out any stones. In a large casserole put the beans, ham hock, carrots, onion, celery, and garlic. Add the water and the bay leaf. Tie the thyme and parsley sprigs together with string and add them to the pot. Bring to a boil, reduce the heat, and simmer gently for 1 hour.

Drain the beans, reserving the cooking liquid. Remove and discard the vegetables, bay leaf, and herb sprigs. Remove the ham hock and set it aside to cool. Season the beans with salt and pepper and set aside until needed. When the ham hock has cooled, remove and chop the meat and set aside until needed.

While the beans are cooking, brown the meats. Rinse the duck pieces and pat dry. Trim off any large pieces of fat and fatty skin. Sprinkle the pieces with salt and pepper. In a large skillet, render the bacon over medium heat until golden. Remove the bacon pieces to paper towels to drain. Brown the duck well in the bacon fat, cooking in batches to avoid crowding the pan, about 15 minutes for each batch. Drain the duck on a plate lined with paper towels. Sprinkle the lamb with salt and pepper and brown it in batches. Drain it on paper towels. Brown the garlic sausage and drain it on paper towels.

When all the meat is browned, pour off all but 4 tablespoons of the fat in the skillet. Add the onions, and sauté until browning, about 10 minutes. Add the garlic and cook another minute. Add the tomatoes, wine, thyme, rosemary, parsley, the reserved ham, and the cooked bacon. Simmer, uncovered, for 10 minutes. Season to taste with salt and pepper.

SERVES 8

1 pound navy beans, soaked overnight
1 meaty ham hock
2 carrots, peeled and halved
1 large onion, halved
1 stalk celery, halved
6 garlic cloves, peeled and slightly crushed
2½ quarts water
1 bay leaf
3 fresh thyme sprigs
4 fresh parsley sprigs
Salt and freshly ground black pepper
1 fresh duck, 4 to 5 pounds, cut up, breast boned, wing tips removed
3 slices thick bacon, diced
1 pound boneless lamb shoulder, fat trimmed, in bite-sized pieces
3 fresh garlic sausages (¾ pound), in bite-sized pieces
2 medium-sized onions, chopped
4 cloves garlic, chopped
2 tomatoes, peeled, seeded, and chopped
¾ cup dry white wine
1 tablespoon fresh thyme leaves, or 1 heaping teaspoon dried thyme
1 tablespoon minced fresh rosemary, or 1 heaping teaspoon dried rosemary
2 tablespoons chopped fresh Italian parsley
1½ cups fresh bread crumbs

Preheat the oven to 350°. Put half the beans in the bottom of a large earthenware pot or ovenproof casserole. Arrange the browned duck, then the lamb and garlic sausage, on top of the beans. Pour the onion and tomato sauce over the top of the meats. Add the other half of the beans, and pour just enough of the cooking liquid from the beans to come almost to the top of the beans. Sprinkle half the bread crumbs evenly over the top. Cook in the preheated oven, uncovered, for 1½ hours. Stir the cassoulet once about halfway through the cooking to incorporate the crust. Sprinkle the top with the remaining bread crumbs and continue cooking. A nicely browned crust should be formed by the end of the cooking time. Serve the cassoulet directly from the pot, giving each person a variety of meats and some of the crust.

GREEK LAMB MEATBALL STEW WITH METAXA AND TWO KINDS OF OLIVES

Metaxa, *a dark brandy from Greece, gives this stew a smoky sweetness that is balanced by tangy Greek olives. Choose the nicest, freshest olives available and, if possible, avoid canned ones, which have a less piquant flavor.*

In a large bowl, mix the lamb, bread crumbs, minced onion, lemon rind, parsley, mint, and egg together, and season with salt and pepper. Shape the meat into balls about the size of a walnut and dust with flour.

Heat the oil in a large pot over medium-high heat and brown the meatballs, in batches, until nicely colored on all sides. Remove to a plate. When all the meatballs are browned, add the red onion and sauté until wilted, about 5 minutes. Add the carrots and sauté another 2 minutes. Add the *metaxa* and cook down quickly, scraping up the browned bits on the bottom of the pan. Add the stock and bring to a boil. Reduce the heat to a slow simmer, and add the browned meatballs, oregano, and both kinds of olives. Simmer covered for 45 minutes. Just before serving, adjust the seasonings and add the parsley. Serve with rice or bread.

SERVES 6

1¾ pounds ground lamb
½ cup fresh bread crumbs
1 small onion, minced
2 heaping teaspoons grated lemon rind
3 tablespoons finely chopped parsley
1 tablespoon finely chopped mint
1 egg, beaten
Salt and freshly ground black pepper
Flour
2 tablespoons olive oil
2 large red onions, halved and sliced
2 carrots, peeled, halved, and sliced into ¼-inch ovals
½ cup *metaxa* (see Pantry)
4 cups chicken stock
½ teaspoon dried oregano
20 kalamata olives (see Pantry), or small black olives
12 cracked green olives
¼ cup chopped Italian parsley

PHO TAI

Pho, *pronounced something like the English word "far," is a very common breakfast soup in Vietnam. It signifies, roughly, "one's own bowl," which is in contrast to the shared, family-style service typical at other meals.* Tai *describes the type of pho, in this case the very common noodle and tender beef combination. As a breakfast meal, this lively dish is very different from what we eat in the West. Hot noodles and steaming broth instantly cook the raw, fresh ingredients that range in flavor from spicy hot to spicy sweet. Pho wakes up the senses; it clears the head and warms the soul. Traditionally it is eaten hot and fast, with the chopsticks in the right hand and a soup spoon in the left. Slurping is allowed and even advocated because it cools the hot noodles on the way into the mouth! Although* pho *is most commonly eaten at breakfast, it is also eaten throughout the day, and* pho *vendors abound in the markets of Vietnam. It requires several hours of preparation (all in the making of the beef stock, a crucial ingredient), but* pho *is worth the time, as it so perfectly demonstrates the distinct and delicious flavors of Vietnamese cooking.*

BEEF STOCK

The unique stock for pho is the backbone of this soup and cannot be reproduced by using canned broth. The stock is best made in advance and can be kept in the refrigerator, covered, for up to three days. One advantage to making the stock ahead is that the fat congeals on the surface of the chilled stock and can be easily removed.

Place the oxtail and beef bones in a large pot and add water to cover. Bring to a boil over high heat. After boiling for a minute or two, drain the bones in a colander and rinse under running water. Rinse out the pot and place the bones back in it with the 6 quarts of water. Bring to a boil.

While the stock water is coming to a boil, char the skins of the onion and ginger by holding them, with tongs, directly over the burner of a gas stove. They can also be charred under a broiler, turning them to blacken all sides. Add the charred onion and ginger to the stock.

Add the cinnamon stick, star anise, bay leaves, peppercorns, *nuoc mam*, and sugar. When the stock begins to boil, reduce the heat to low and simmer, uncovered, for 3 hours. Skim the top of the stock occasionally. Strain the stock through a colander lined with cheesecloth. Allow to cool, skimming off all the fat that rises to the top.

SERVES 4

BEEF STOCK

2½ pounds oxtails
2 pounds beef bone, in pieces
6 quarts water
1 large onion, papery outer skin removed
3-inch piece unpeeled ginger
1 cinnamon stick
5 whole star anise (see Pantry)
2 bay leaves
15 black peppercorns
3 tablespoons *nuoc mam* (see Pantry)
1 tablespoon sugar

PHO

1 pound fresh *bahn pho*, or dried
   rice noodles or sticks (see
   Pantry)
2 quarts beef stock (see recipe)
¼ cup *nuoc mam* (see Pantry)
½ pound tenderloin beef, sliced
   paper thin
4 green onions, roots trimmed,
   white part and some of the
   green leaves sliced diagonally
8 sprigs fresh cilantro (see Pantry)
2 cups mung bean sprouts, rinsed
   and drained
4 small fresh hot red or green
   chilies (see Pantry), sliced
   diagonally
4 large sprigs fresh basil
1 lime, sliced into 4 wedges

PHO

Once the beef stock is made, assembling the soup is very easy and fast, since the stock "cooks" the other ingredients right in the bowl. The beef is much easier to slice if it has been partially frozen (for a half hour or so), or have the butcher slice it for you.

If using dried rice noodles, soak them in warm water for 20 minutes (fresh noodles do not need to soak). Heat the beef stock over medium heat and keep warm until needed. Bring a large pot of water to a boil.

While the noodles are soaking and the water is coming to a boil, prepare and arrange the soup ingredients. Bring the beef stock to a boil and add the *nuoc mam*. Arrange the sliced beef, green onions, and cilantro on a platter and cover with plastic.

On a separate platter, arrange the mung bean sprouts, chilies, basil sprigs, and lime wedges. These are passed at the table, to be added to the soup by each diner.

Drain the rice noodles in a colander. Drop them in the boiling water, stir once, and drain them again. Divide the warm noodles among 4 large soup bowls. On top of the noodles, arrange equal amounts of first beef, then green onions and cilantro. Ladle the boiling beef stock over the beef and noodles; the stock will cook the paper-thin slices of beef on contact. Serve the soup immediately, while it is very hot. Each person can add bean sprouts, chilies, basil leaves, and lime juice to his or her liking.

PERSIAN STEW WITH GAME HENS AND SOUR CHERRIES

*P*oultry *is widely popular throughout the Middle East, both for its versatility and its economy. In this dish the hens are cooked long enough to melt off the bone, and the meat can be eaten with the fingers, or with pita bread to both pinch up a bite and soak up the fragrant sauce. Middle Eastern cooking often combines savory and sweet or tangy flavors, and the aroma can be as critical to the finished dish as the taste. Serve these stewed game hens with warmed pita bread or steamed basmati rice.*

Cut the game hens in half along the backbone and the breastbone. Trim off any excess fat. Sprinkle the hens with flour and tap off the excess. Heat 2 tablespoons of the oil in a large pot and brown the hen halves, two at a time, over medium heat, adding the rest of the oil as necessary. Set aside on a plate until needed.

When all the hens are browned, add the onions to the pan and sauté them until wilted and browning, about 10 minutes. Add the garlic and sauté another minute. Add the coriander, cinnamon, cumin, ginger, and cardamom and sauté another minute, until aromatic. Add the chicken stock and sour cherries and bring to a boil. Reduce the heat. Arrange the hens in a single layer in the pot, spoon some of the sauce over them, and simmer, covered, until very tender, about 1 hour. Turn the hens over once or twice while they are cooking, and add salt and pepper to taste.

While the hens are cooking, toast the almonds in a 400° oven until just beginning to color. Combine the parsley, cilantro, and green onions. Serve the hens with the minced greens and toasted almonds on top.

SERVES 4

2 large (1¾ pound each) Rock Cornish game hens
3 tablespoons flour
3 tablespoons olive oil
3 onions, halved and sliced
4 garlic cloves, minced to a paste
2 teaspoons ground coriander
1 teaspoon ground cinnamon
1 teaspoon ground cumin
½ teaspoon ground ginger
½ teaspoon ground cardamom
1½ cups chicken stock, low salt, defatted
1 cup dried sour cherries (see Pantry)
Salt and freshly ground black pepper, to taste
½ cup blanched slivered almonds
¼ bunch parsley, minced
¼ bunch cilantro (see Pantry), minced
3 green onions, white part and ⅓ of the green leaves, finely chopped

Opposite page, lower left: Persian Stew with Game Hens and Sour Cherries; top right: Gardener's Vegetable Mélange (recipe on page 90)

GARDENER'S VEGETABLE MÉLANGE

This is truly a fresh vegetable stew, meant to be adapted to whatever may be growing in the garden or what is in season at the local farmer's market or the produce stand. The vegetables should be cooked enough to be tender but not mushy, so their freshness stands out. With its combination of utterly fresh vegetables, French herbs, and crunchy, garlicky croutons sprinkled with salty pecorino cheese, this stew is alive with well-defined flavors and varied textures. (RECIPE PHOTO ON PAGE 89, TOP RIGHT)

Drop the baby onions into boiling water and parboil for 3 minutes. Remove and cool until easy to handle. Trim off just the roots, leaving the tops intact. Peel off the papery skins.

Heat the olive oil in a large pot over medium heat, and sauté the onions and leeks until browning, about 5 minutes. Add the zucchini, crookneck squash, eggplants, carrots, and kohlrabi and sauté another 5 minutes. Add the corn kernels and vegetable broth, and bring to a boil. Reduce the heat and add the tarragon, thyme, parsley, and salt and pepper to taste. Simmer, covered, for 15 minutes, or until the vegetables are tender.

While the vegetables are cooking, prepare the croutons. Slice the bread into 1/2-inch-thick slices. Toast the slices, and immediately brush one side of each slice with olive oil. Rub the oiled side lightly with the cut end of the garlic clove.

When the vegetables are tender, adjust the seasonings. Spoon the stew into 4 large ovenproof bowls, arrange 1 or 2 croutons on top, and sprinkle with grated pecorino cheese. Run the bowls under the broiler to melt the cheese, and serve immediately. Serve the remaining croutons on the side.

SERVES 4

½ pound baby onions or cipollini (see Pantry)

3 tablespoons olive oil, plus additional oil for croutons

2 leeks, white part only, sliced into ¼-inch rounds

2 small zucchini, sliced into ¼-inch rounds

2 small crookneck squash, sliced into ½-inch chunks

3 small Japanese eggplants, sliced into ½-inch rounds

2 medium-sized carrots, sliced into ½-inch rounds

2 kohlrabi, peeled down to the white flesh and sliced into ½-inch chunks

Kernels from 1 ear of corn

3 cups vegetable broth

1 heaping teaspoon chopped fresh tarragon, or ½ teaspoon dried tarragon

1 heaping teaspoon fresh thyme leaves, or ½ teaspoon dried thyme

1 heaping tablespoon chopped fresh Italian parsley

Salt and freshly ground black pepper, to taste

1 loaf crusty French or Italian bread

1 garlic clove, peeled and root end trimmed

¼ cup freshly grated pecorino cheese (see Pantry)

GOLDEN BIRIYANI

SERVES 6

2 cups good-quality basmati rice
   (see Pantry)
1 tablespoon salt
4 garlic cloves, peeled and root
   ends trimmed
1-inch piece fresh ginger, peeled
   and sliced
4 to 6 hot green chilies, such as
   serranos or jalapeños (see
   Pantry)
¼ teaspoon cayenne pepper
1¼ teaspoons ground coriander
1 teaspoon ground cumin
1 teaspoon ground cinnamon
1 teaspoon ground turmeric
Seeds from 6 cardamom pods,
   cracked open
2 bay leaves
1½ teaspoons salt
1 cup plain yogurt
2 tablespoons ghee (see Pantry), or
   butter
2 tablespoons vegetable oil
2 half chicken breasts, boned,
   skinned, and cut into bite-sized
   pieces
2 chicken thighs, boned, skinned,
   and cut into bite-sized pieces

Biriyani is a classic Indian dish, usually reserved for important occasions and celebrations. It is of Mogul origin. The Moguls were nomads from Mongolia who brought with them into India the influences of Persian cuisine and who over time established a "courtly" style of cooking that combined indigenous Indian foods with their ecumenical cuisine. Biriyani is a hearty meal, best served with several types of chutney (mango chutney is a must!), raita, and assorted Indian breads.

In a large bowl, rinse the rice in several changes of lukewarm water, agitating the rice with your hands. The water should be mostly clear. Fill the bowl again and add the salt. Soak the rice while you bring a large pot of water to a boil. Drain the rice, add it to the boiling water and cook until just tender, about 5 minutes. Drain in a colander and rinse under lukewarm water. Shake out the excess water and set aside until needed.

Preheat the oven to 350°. In a blender, grind the garlic, ginger, chilies, cayenne, coriander, cumin, cinnamon, turmeric, cardamom seeds, bay leaves, salt, and yogurt into a smooth paste. Set aside until needed.

In a large skillet, heat the ghee and vegetable oil over medium heat. Brown the chicken well on all sides and remove to a plate. In the same pan, sauté the onions until browning, about 10 minutes. Remove to a plate. Sauté the cauliflower until lightly seared, about 3 minutes, and remove. Add the yogurt paste, stirring well until it is bubbly, aromatic, and nearly evaporated. Add the ¾ cup of water and mix well. Add the chicken, two-thirds of the onions, the cauliflower, and the sweet potatoes. Cover and simmer until the potatoes are just tender, about 20 minutes.

(CONTINUED ON NEXT PAGE)

Use ½ tablespoon of the butter to butter a large, deep baking dish. Layer half the rice in the bottom, then all of the chicken and vegetable mixture, then the rest of the rice. Put the remaining one-third of the onions on the top. In a small saucepan, bring the ½ cup of water and the remaining 2½ tablespoons of butter to a boil, and boil until the butter foams. Remove from the heat, stir in the saffron, and pour slowly over the top of the rice casserole, distributing evenly. Cover tightly with aluminum foil, and bake for 45 minutes. Remove the aluminum foil, sprinkle the cashews and raisins over the top, and cook another 15 minutes, uncovered. Just before serving, sprinkle the cilantro over the dish and serve with raita on the side.

CUCUMBER RAITA

This cooling cucumber relish is a good foil for the spicy biriyani.

With a fork, beat the yogurt until smooth. Stir in the cucumber, cumin, and mint. Season with salt and pepper, sprinkle with paprika, and refrigerate until needed.

1½ large yellow onions, halved and thinly sliced
½ head cauliflower, cored and divided into florets
¾ cup water
2 small sweet potatoes, peeled and diced
3 tablespoons butter
Scant ½ cup water
¼ teaspoon crushed saffron threads (see Pantry)
½ cup cashews, toasted and halved
½ cup golden raisins
Chopped fresh cilantro (see Pantry)
Cucumber Raita (see recipe, below)

CUCUMBER RAITA
2 cups plain yogurt
1 cucumber, peeled and grated
½ teaspoon ground cumin
4 mint leaves, minced
Salt and freshly ground black pepper, to taste
Paprika

PAELLA

Paella is at its heart a rustic dish, designed for cooking the day's fresh catch on the beach over coals. It is one of those excellent dishes that evolved from a simple template of rice, olive oil, seafood, and saffron into a rich and varied catchall of the best ingredients. Paella originated in the Spanish province of Valencia, with its fertile coast and abundant waters. Once you follow its basic pattern, paella can be filled out with whatever is fresh or in season or just favored by the cook, so make replacements and adjustments accordingly. Paella, named for the pot—the paellera—in which it is made, is "dry cooked" (cooked uncovered) so that each grain of rice stays separate and whole, not sticky.

Preheat the oven to 350°. Heat 1 tablespoon of the oil over medium heat in a 15-inch paellera or a very large skillet. Pull the casing off the chorizo and cook the sausage until crumbly, about 7 minutes. Remove with a slotted spoon. Add another tablespoon of oil. Sauté the shrimp with 1 of the minced garlic cloves until bright pink and opaque, about 3 minutes; remove. Add the remaining 2 tablespoons of olive oil to the pan. Sprinkle the chicken pieces with salt and pepper and brown them until golden, 10 minutes per side. Remove to paper towels to drain.

Sauté the onion and pepper until the onion is browning, about 10 minutes. Add the remaining 3 cloves of minced garlic and sauté another minute. Add the rice and stir until it begins to turn opaque, about 3 minutes. Stir in the chicken stock, chicken, chorizo, asparagus tips, thyme, saffron, and paprika, and add plenty of salt and pepper to taste. Give the pan a shake to settle the rice, and bring the liquid to a boil. Do not stir again. Simmer the paella until the liquid is at the top of the rice and the surface is beginning to develop steam holes, 10 to 12 minutes.

Arrange the shrimp, mussels, and clams on top, and put the paella in the preheated oven. Cook another 20 minutes or so. The paella is done when the rice is tender and dry. Remove from the oven and let the paella rest, covered lightly with a dishcloth, for 5 minutes. Discard any clams or mussels that do not open. Sprinkle the paella with chopped parsley and serve in the paellera.

SERVES 8

4 tablespoons olive oil
½ pound chorizo (see Pantry)
16 medium shrimp, in the shell
4 garlic cloves, minced
2½- to 3-pound chicken, cut into 12 pieces, wing tips removed
Salt and freshly ground black pepper, to taste
1 large red onion, chopped
1 red bell pepper, seeded and chopped
3 cups short-grain white rice, such as Arborio (see Pantry)
6 cups chicken stock, low salt, defatted
30 asparagus spears, top 4 inches only
1 tablespoon fresh thyme leaves, or 1 teaspoon dried thyme
¼ teaspoon crushed saffron threads (see Pantry)
1½ teaspoons sweet (Spanish or Hungarian) paprika
10 mussels, scrubbed and debearded
10 clams, scrubbed
2 tablespoons chopped Italian parsley

Opposite page: Paella, top left; lower left: Duck with Pears and Figs (recipe on page 96)

DUCK WITH PEARS AND FIGS

Anec amb Peres y Figues *shows the unique flavors of Spain's Catalonia region at their finest. When savory and sweet are combined in this subtle way, each brings out the other—nothing is lost or muted. Serve this dish on a bed of garlicky mashed potatoes or with plain boiled rice.* (RECIPE PHOTO ON PAGE 95, LOWER LEFT)

Put the figs in a bowl with the sherry and set aside until needed.

Preheat the oven to 425°. Trim the fat from the duck, reserving 1 chunk of fat (about a 1-inch cube). Cut off the last joint of the wings and set aside with the neck, back (if not meaty enough to roast), and giblets (discard the liver). Sprinkle the duck pieces with salt and pepper and roast them in the preheated oven for 1 hour, turning once.

While the duck is roasting, render the chunk of duck fat in a saucepan over medium-low heat. Brown the reserved duck parts and giblets. Pour off the excess fat. Add the water and the 3 whole shallots, the carrot, celery, parsley sprigs, thyme sprig, bay leaf, cinnamon stick, and peppercorns. Bring to a boil, then reduce the heat and simmer, uncovered, for 45 minutes.

When the duck pieces are cooked, remove them from the roasting pan and discard the fat. Put the roasting pan on a burner over medium heat and pour in the sherry and figs, scraping up the browned bits on the bottom of the pan. Reduce the liquid for 2 minutes, and set aside until needed.

SERVES 4

10 dried figs, quartered
1 cup Amontillado, or other dry Spanish sherry
4½- to 5-pound duck, with neck and giblets, cut up
Salt and freshly ground black pepper
3 cups water
4 shallots, 3 peeled whole, 1 minced
1 carrot, halved
1 celery stalk, halved
2 sprigs fresh Italian parsley
1 sprig fresh thyme
1 bay leaf
1 cinnamon stick
10 peppercorns
2 tablespoons butter
1 garlic clove, minced
1 tablespoon flour
3 pears, peeled, cored, and quartered
Fresh thyme leaves, for garnish

In a large casserole, heat 1 tablespoon of the butter and cook the remaining minced shallot over medium heat until wilted, about 5 minutes. Add the garlic and cook 1 minute. Strain the giblet broth into the pot, and add the sherry and figs from the roasting pan. With your fingers, mash together the remaining tablespoon of butter with the flour, and add this, bit by bit, to the sauce, whisking between additions. Simmer the sauce for 10 minutes, until thickened and smooth. Season to taste with salt and pepper.

Arrange the duck pieces in the pot with the sauce, add the pears, and cover. Simmer over very low heat for 20 minutes, or until the pears are tender. Sprinkle each serving with fresh thyme leaves.

ORANGE-CHILI CHICKEN WITH BLACK BEANS

This easy chicken dish combines the sweetness of oranges with the spiciness of hot chilies. It is surprising combinations such as this that characterize some of the best cooking of Mexico and New Mexico. Use any of the hot chili sauces available in the market. Serve this dish with rice or hot corn tortillas and with such condiments as avocado, chopped cilantro, sour cream, and sliced red onion marinated in lime juice.

Heat the oil in a large skillet over medium heat. Brown the chicken pieces well on all sides, cooking them in batches to avoid crowding. Remove to a plate lined with paper towels and allow to drain. In the same skillet, cook the onion until wilted and browning, about 8 minutes. Add the garlic and cook another minute.

Put the browned chicken back into the skillet and add the orange juice, chicken stock, and chili sauce. Cover and simmer over low heat for 30 minutes. Add the black beans with 2 tablespoons of their liquid (if canned) and the red pepper strips. Simmer, uncovered, another 30 minutes. Add the rum and salt, to taste, and simmer 15 more minutes. Sprinkle with cilantro and serve.

SERVES 4 TO 6

2 tablespoons olive oil
1 whole chicken, 3 to 4 pounds, cut up and skinned
1 large red onion, halved and thinly sliced
4 garlic cloves, minced
1½ cups fresh-squeezed orange juice
¾ cup chicken stock
3 teaspoons hot chili sauce, or to taste
1¾ cup cooked black beans
1 red bell pepper, sliced into strips
1 tablespoon dark rum
Salt, to taste
Chopped fresh cilantro leaves (see Pantry)

RED POZOLE

This hearty Mexican soup from Guadalajara is made of hominy and pork, made "red" with dried red chilies. Because it is an easy and informal dish, pozole is traditionally prepared in large quantities and served to family and friends for parties and holidays. Pozole should be accompanied by bowls of condiments to sprinkle on top; possibilities include shredded lettuce or cabbage, chopped onion, lime wedges (a must), sliced radishes, chopped fresh oregano, chopped cilantro, avocado, salsa, chopped green chilies, hot chili sauce, or crispy fried tortillas. In this recipe the customary pig's feet and salt pork are omitted to make the dish less fatty, but the soup bones are retained to give the soup full flavor.

In a very large soup pot, combine the pork, soup bones, garlic head, water, and salt. Stud the onion with the cloves and add to the pot. Bring very slowly to a gentle boil, skimming off any foam that rises to the top. Agitate the meat and bones once or twice to bring the foam to the surface. Reduce the heat and simmer over very low, covered, for 1 hour.

Meanwhile, put the dried red chilies in a bowl and add boiling water to cover. Soak for 30 minutes. Put the softened chilies and ⅓ cup of the soaking liquid in a blender with the chipotle chilies and the garlic cloves. Purée until smooth. Set aside until needed.

When the meat has cooked for 1 hour, remove the garlic head, onion, and soup bones and discard. Pour the puréed chilies into the pot. Add the hominy, oregano, and cumin and continue to simmer, uncovered, for 45 minutes. Season to taste with salt and pepper. Serve pozole with plenty of condiments.

SERVES 12

2¼ pounds boneless pork shouder, cut into bite-sized pieces
2¼ pounds pork soup bones
1 whole head garlic, unpeeled, top third sliced off
4 quarts water
Large pinch of salt
1 large onion, peeled and ends trimmed
5 whole cloves
3 dried mild red chilies, seeded, such as New Mexico, pasilla, or guajillo (see Pantry)
1½ chipotle chilies, from canned adobo sauce (see Pantry)
3 garlic cloves, peeled
46 ounces canned hominy, drained
1½ teaspoons dried oregano
¼ teaspoon ground cumin
Salt and freshly ground black pepper, to taste
Condiments

Opposite page, lower left: Red Pozole; top right: Arroz Verde con Pollo (recipe on page 102)

ARROZ VERDE CON POLLO

The marriage of chicken and rice in one stovetop pot is an enduring one, and a much extrapolated one as well. Nothing is more basic than cooking these two together for a hearty, easy meal, but the experience can become as complex as the cook wants to make it. Green rice—full of the flavors of mild, smoky green chilies, onion, and cilantro—is an aromatic and fresh-tasting variation on the more traditional red rice with tomato and saffron. Add jalapeño for a hotter dish. (RECIPE PHOTO ON PAGE 101, TOP RIGHT)

Thoroughly char the chilies over the burner of a gas stove or under a broiler. Place the blackened chilies in a paper bag for 10 minutes to cool and steam them. Scrape off the blackened skin and remove the stems, seeds, and veins. Set aside 1 of the chilies for garnish.

In a blender, purée the 5 remaining chilies with the onion, garlic, cilantro, lime juice, and water. Rinse the rice under running water in a large sieve or colander until the water runs clear. Set aside to drain, shaking periodically to remove any excess water.

In a large casserole with a tight-fitting lid, heat the oil. Brown the chicken pieces over medium heat until golden brown, about 10 minutes per side. Remove to a plate to drain. Lower the heat and sauté the rice until opaque, about 2 minutes, scraping up some of the browned bits from the bottom of the pan. Add the chili-and-onion purée and cook until aromatic, 1 minute or so, scraping up the rest of the browned bits. Season with salt. Add the chicken pieces. Add 2½ cups of the chicken stock, stir well, and bring to a boil. Reduce the heat to medium low and cook, uncovered, for 10 minutes. Cover tightly and cook over low heat until the chicken and rice are tender and the liquid absorbed, about 20 minutes, adding some of the reserved stock if the rice gets too dry.

When the chicken and rice are done, remove the pot from the heat, place a double layer of paper towels under the lid, cover again, and allow the rice to rest for 10 minutes. Chop the reserved chili and sprinkle it over the dish, along with the cilantro leaves.

SERVES 6

6 mild long green chilies, such as Anaheims (see Pantry)
1 onion, coarsely chopped
3 garlic cloves
1 bunch cilantro (see Pantry), long stems removed
Juice of 1 lime
½ cup water
2 cups long-grain white rice
3 tablespoons olive oil
1 chicken, 3½ pounds, cut into pieces, or 8 chicken thighs
Salt, to taste
3 cups chicken stock, low salt, defatted
Fresh cilantro leaves, for garnish

NONYA LAKSA

SERVES 6

REMPAH OR SPICE BLEND

2 stalks lemongrass (see Pantry),
   using 2 inches above the root,
   chopped
2 shallots, peeled and
   chopped
2 garlic cloves, halved
2 small fresh red chilies, or
   to taste
¾-inch cube fresh galangal
   (see Pantry), peeled and
   sliced
1 teaspoon blacan (see
   Pantry)
3 tablespoons Malaysian
   curry powder (see Pantry)
1 teaspoon turmeric
½ teaspoon sugar
⅓ cup vegetable oil

This delicious dish from Malaysia is a perfect representative of that country's rich and varied culinary history. Laksa, a delicate noodle and coconut soup, combines Malay spices with Chinese noodles. It originated within the Nonya culture, or "Straits-born" Chinese, wealthy traders who settled on the Malaysian peninsula centuries ago and established a unique cultural identity. Malaysian cuisine also shows the profound influence of Indian cooking, brought by merchants from that country who had long exchanged their goods. And a touch of European flavor marks Malaysian cuisine because the Portuguese, in the mid-16th century, controlled the profitable peninsula. Laksa requires time but is worth the effort. This version comes from the Nonyas of Malacca, where coconut milk is a central ingredient.

Put all the ingredients for the rempah except the oil in a food processor or blender and process until well minced. With the motor running, add the oil in a thin stream and continue to process until a smooth paste is formed.

Bring a large pot of water to a boil.

Meanwhile, in a pot over medium-low heat, cook the rempah, stirring constantly, until oily, about 4 minutes. Add 1 cup of the thick coconut milk. Continue to cook, stirring constantly, until the mixture is thick, 10 minutes. Remove 8 tablespoons of the mixture and set aside.

To the remaining paste in the pot, add the other 2 cups of coconut milk and the water, mixing well to combine. Bring to a boil. Reduce the heat to very low and add the chicken, broccoli, and tofu. Cook over low heat, just the slightest simmer, for 5 minutes. Add the shrimp and cook another 5 minutes. Season with salt.

(CONTINUED NEXT PAGE)

LAKSA

Rempah (see page 103)
3 cups thick coconut milk
  (see Pantry)
4 cups water
3 half chicken breasts,
  skinned, boned, and cut
  into bite-sized pieces
¾ pound Chinese broccoli
  (see Pantry), trimmed and
  sliced into 4-inch lengths
Fried tofu (see Pantry), sliced
  lengthwise into ¼-inch
  slices
24 medium-sized shrimp,
  shelled and deveined
Salt, to taste
⅔ pound dried rice sticks (see
  Pantry)
6 ounces bean sprouts, rinsed
2 green onions, white part and
  some of the green, thinly
  sliced on the diagonal
2 limes, sliced into wedges
Sambal (see Pantry)

Drop the noodles into the boiling water, cook for 1 minute, and drain in a colander.

Divide the bean sprouts between 6 large soup bowls. Divide the noodles and place them on the bean sprouts. Ladle soup into each bowl and sprinkle with sliced green onion. Serve with lime wedges and a sambal of your choice on the side.

INDEX